THE WARRIOR MINDSET FOR SUCCESS

THE WARRIOR MINDSET FOR SUCCESS

ESSENTIAL STRATEGIES FOR ACHIEVING YOUR GOALS

BRIAN TRACY

Published 2025 by Gildan Media LLC
aka G&D Media
www.GandDmedia.com

THE WARRIOR MINDSET FOR SUCCESS. Copyright © 2025 by Brian Tracy. All rights reserved.

No part of this book may be used, reproduced or transmitted in any manner whatsoever, by any means (electronic, photocopying, recording, or otherwise), without the prior written permission of the author, except in the case of brief quotations embodied in critical articles and reviews. No liability is assumed with respect to the use of the information contained within. Although every precaution has been taken, the author and publisher assume no liability for errors or omissions. Neither is any liability assumed for damages resulting from the use of the information contained herein.

Front cover design by David Rheinhardt of Pyrographx

Interior design by Meghan Day Healey of Story Horse, LLC

Library of Congress Cataloging-in-Publication Data is available upon request

ISBN: 978-1-7225-0708-4

10 9 8 7 6 5 4 3 2 1

Contents

Introduction 7

1 The Principle of the Objective 21

2 The Offensive 29

3 Simplify! 47

4 The Power of Concentration 67

5 Unity of Command 85

6 Gather Intelligence 103

Introduction

Put up your tray table, straighten your seat back, and fasten your seatbelt, because we are now entering into the most exciting time in all of human history. Because you are reading this book, you have a front row seat. You are at the head of the line, at the front of the crowd.

In the months ahead, you are going to have more, do more, and be more than perhaps you may have ever imagined possible. We are entering into the golden age of mankind, and you are uniquely positioned to enjoy the rewards and possibilities of this age.

Let's begin by asking, how can you tell who a person really is? How can you determine what kind of a person you are talking to? How can you determine their true values, beliefs, and goals? Is it by what they say, by what they intend, by what they hope, plan, wish, or dream about? Is it by what they say or write or what they promise when they run for public office? How can you tell who a person really is?

The answer is simple: you can only tell who a person really is by looking at what they do. It is not what you wish or hope or intend that counts, but only what you actually do on a day-to-day basis, and especially what you do under pressure. Fewer than 10 percent of adults read books, attend courses, and listen to audio programs.

These 10 percent own the future. These 10 percent who will know what they need to know and do what they need to do to become masters of change rather than victims.

Since you are reading this book, you are obviously among that top 10 percent—not because of what you wish or hope or intend, but because of what you are doing right now. You are members of the talented tenth. You are a member of an elite. You don't wait for things to happen; you make them happen. You don't hope for opportunities; you go out and create your own opportunities. You don't follow the paths left by others; you go where there is no path and blaze your own trail. The very act of committing yourself to continual learning moves you to the front of the line, enabling you to take full control over your destiny.

Many years ago, as a young man growing up poor without any education or skills, I began asking why some people are more successful than others. I've spent decades, I've read hundreds and thousands of books and articles, I have listened to thousands of hours of audio programs and spent thousands of hours in courses and seminars seeking the answer to this simple question: why are some people more successful than others?

Perhaps the greatest discovery in the science of success was articulated by the American philosopher Ralph Waldo Emerson more than 150 years ago. He said, "A man becomes what he thinks about most of the time." Similarly, in the twentieth century, inspirational speaker Earl Nightingale revolutionized an entire generation with what he called the "strangest secret" of success: you become what you think about.

Everything you are and everything you ever will be is determined by the way you think. If you change the quality of your thinking, you will change the quality of your life. You've heard the old saying: if you sow a thought, you reap an action; if you sow an action, you reap a habit; if you sow a habit, you reap a character; and if you sow a character, you reap a destiny.

To put it another way, you may not be what you think you are—but what you think, you are. All causation in your life is mental. You are where and what you are because of the way you think. You have attracted everything in your life by your dominant thoughts.

The good news is that you can have more and be more, because you can change the person you are. You can change the things you think about and the way you think about those things. If you change the way you think, your destiny and your potential can become unlimited.

You are not only what you do; you are how you think. If you think in a clear, calm, constructive, and positive way towards yourself and others, your external world will be organized, successful, and characterized by high achievement. If on the other hand you think in a negative, angry, confused, or unrealistic way, your external world will be a continual succession of problems.

In every case, you are free to choose. Only you can choose the thoughts you think. By choosing those thoughts, you choose your emotions and consequently your actions, and by choosing your thoughts, emotions, and actions, you create your entire world.

Perhaps the most important factor in our lives today is the speed and impact of change. Information in every field is doubling every two to three years. This means that you must double your knowledge and skill every two to three years just to stay even. Technology is exploding in all directions. As Andrew Grove of Intel observed, the first law of technology is that anything that can be done by technology *will* be done by technology, and probably sooner rather than later.

Simultaneous with the growth of technology and the explosion of information is the proliferation of competition in every field. Because of this aggressive competition, you'll have to become smarter and better every week, every month, every year, just to stay even. To enjoy the wonderful life that is possible for you, you'll have to continually outthink and leapfrog your competition locally, nationwide, and worldwide.

The purpose of this book is to give you the tools that you need to survive and thrive in the exciting months and years ahead. It is to give you a set of special skills and insights practiced by the most successful men and women of our time.

When you think the way the most successful people think, you will act the way the most successful people act, and you'll get the results that the most successful people get. In the early twentieth century, the great British historian Arnold Toynbee wrote a multi-volume study of civilizations and history throughout the ages. He studied the life cycles of twenty-eight great civilizations to find out what they had in common. His central conclusion was very important, and it applies to your life today.

Toynbee developed what he called the "challenge and response" theory of history. He found that every large civilization began as a small group or tribe of people who were confronted with a challenge from the outside, usually a challenge from other hostile peoples. In order to survive, the small group had to respond to this challenge. If it responded effectively, it would conquer its enemy and grow stronger. In this process, it would come up against another enemy and would again be challenged from the outside. In order to survive, the group again had to respond effectively. If it did, it would conquer its enemy and grow stronger. Again, however, in growing larger and stronger, it would be challenged by another enemy from the outside. If the growing tribe responded effectively to the larger challenge, it would again continue to grow and eventually collide with yet another challenge that would force it to respond again, in this case differently. As long as the tribe continued to respond effectively to the inevitable challenges of survival and growth, it continued to grow stronger, until the most successful tribes formed empires, kingdoms, and ultimately civilizations.

The German philosopher Friedrich Nietzsche once wrote, "Whatever doesn't destroy me makes me stronger." Whatever applies to individuals usually applies to groups of individuals as well, including companies and other organizations.

Your life is a continual succession of problems, difficulties, obstacles, defeats, disappointments, and challenges. They never end. They start in early childhood, and they continue throughout your life. Despite your best efforts to avoid them, they come anyway, unbidden.

The only thing over which you have any control is the way you respond to these challenges. If you respond effectively, you continue to grow and become stronger. If you respond ineffectively, the challenges can overwhelm you and cause you emotional, physical, and financial setbacks, if not complete reversals.

Your job, then, is to respond effectively to the inevitable challenges that you will face throughout your life. The better and more constructively you think, the stronger and more powerful you'll become in responding to the inevitable difficulties that life will throw at you.

In a popular movie, there is a scene where the new young executive is given a major and difficult assignment his first day on the job. He turns to his boss and asks, "Is this a test?" His boss looks him in the eye and answers, "Isn't everything?"

It's a great observation. Everything in life is a test. Every problem or difficulty you have is a test. Every large or small crisis you face is a test. Every challenge with your customers, your finances, your business, and your future is a test. The only question is, how well do you respond? Do you rise to the challenge and meet it effectively, or do you allow it to overwhelm you? Do you become calm, cool, and creative, or do you become angry, upset, and frustrated?

The challenge is inevitable. The response is always up to you.

Most people function in what is called the *reactive responsive mode*. They react unthinkingly to things that happen to them and around them. They respond emotionally and angrily to frustration, setbacks, and difficulties. Instead of taking the time to stop, think, and respond in an effective and constructive way, they allow events to overwhelm them like waves from the ocean.

However, the men and women who reach positions of responsibility in our society—leaders at every level—are those who have developed the quality of thoughtfulness. They have learned how to think better and more effectively than the average person, and this brings us to one of the most important principles of success. It is called *the law of integrative complexity.* This law says that in any group, the individual who is able to integrate the greatest amount of information and make effective decisions based on that information will eventually come to dominate all the others in that group.

How effective and intelligent you are as a human being is largely determined by how well you can integrate different pieces of information that enable you to analyze and make good decisions upon which to act. This is why people with more experience are usually far more effective than people with less experience. They have more individual pieces of information to work with when facing a new situation, which may have parallels with previous situations. In the Civil War, after his Confederate forces had won a series of important victories against superior Union forces, General Robert E. Lee said, "The only thing I fear is that the Union will field a general against me who thinks better than I do."

General Norman Schwarzkopf, who achieved a stunning victory in the Gulf War in 1991, served at every level of the U.S. Army for thirty years before being appointed commander-in-chief of the Gulf forces. He had the best training in the world and some of the finest and most in-depth experience possible for a commanding officer. When he took over the forces in the Gulf War, he was prepared to completely outthink his opponents in every area.

Your job, your goal, is to be a leader. Your job is to rise to the top of your organization and to be a leader in your business, your family, and your community. Your job is to make a significant contribution to yourself and the people who rely on you. Your job is to become all you can be, to continually grow and become better and better and increasingly valuable to yourself and others.

In 1962, top aeronautical engineers were saying that it was impossible for a plane to go faster than the speed of sound. They said that there was an invisible wall in the sky at the speed of sound and that if a plane attempted to exceed this speed, it would hit the wall and disintegrate, and the pilot would be killed. However, they had not reckoned on one factor: the great test pilot Chuck Yeager didn't believe them. He believed that this wall was imaginary, that it was a myth, and that if he flew fast enough, he would go straight through it into smooth air on the other side, and that's exactly what he did. As he went through the sound barrier, the sound of the sonic boom crashed across the desert floor, and another myth about human limitations was destroyed forever.

For the next twenty-five years, the experts all agreed that although it may have been possible that an airplane flying at high altitude with a limited amount of friction could go faster than the speed of sound, it was impossible for any machine to do that on the ground. For twenty-five years, people tried and failed countless times to break the sound barrier on the ground. Then in 1997, a daring driver with a supersonic car lined it up, put the pedal to the metal, broke the sound barrier on earth, and set the greatest land speed record in history. Another mental, emotional, physical, spiritual, and psychological barrier had been broken.

It's time for you to break your success barriers as well. Do you want to be financially independent? Well, then, why aren't you? More people are becoming millionaires today at a faster rate than ever before in human history. Somewhere, somehow, every four and a half minutes, twenty-four hours a day, seven days a week, 365 days a year, someone becomes a self-made millionaire in America. We now have self-made millionaires, multimillionaires, billionaires, and even multibillionaires. Most of the richest men in America today, if not the world, have become wealthy starting with nothing. In fact, most self-made millionaires had nothing or less than nothing when they started out.

Economists are sometimes said to be the people who have predicted eighteen of the last two recessions. The world is full of negative thinkers, naysayers, critics, complainers, and failures who will go to great lengths to tell you that success is no longer possible in America. They will tell you that it's not what you know, it's *whom* you know. They will tell you that success is a matter of dishonesty or luck or a combination of both. These people delight in pointing out the occasional businessperson each year who is accused of dishonest activities. They ignore the millions of honest, hardworking men and women who are doing extraordinary things in their financial lives, usually starting from nothing at all.

Most self-made millionaires in America have been broke or nearly broke more than three times. Most self-made millionaires in America have worked ten, fifteen, and twenty years to achieve financial independence. It has never been more possible for you to achieve your financial goals than it is here and now in our economy, with the opportunities that are surrounding you on all sides. Around the turn of the twentieth century, the great Harvard psychologist William James wrote, "The greatest revolution of my generation is the discovery that individuals, by changing their inner attitudes of mind, can change the outer aspects of their lives."

All causation is mental. When you decide to crash through your own success barriers, you'll find that virtually all of your limits existed largely in your imagination. Your greatest obstacles to success are not outside of yourself, but inside yourself. It is the way you think and feel about your possibilities that largely determines what they are and what you become with them.

The greatest barriers to success and achievement have always been the twin enemies of fear and doubt. Fear is the biggest obstacle of all, and fear generates the doubt that holds you back. Fear of failure, fear of loss, of poverty, of ridicule, of embarrassment—fears of all kinds cause us to put our feet on our own brakes and make excuses instead of making progress. Self-doubt, the failure to believe in your own abilities, fed by fears of all kinds, holds you back from even trying, and fear and doubt work together in your conscious mind to generate rationalizations and justifications for underachievement and failure. Fear and doubt cause you to sell yourself short and feel inferior to others, thinking they are better or smarter than you, when in reality they're just using their talents more effectively than you are.

Here's the truth: no one is smarter than you, and no one is better than you. You are as good and as smart as anyone you will ever meet, but people are like bodybuilders. Every human has the same 610 muscles as Arnold Schwarzenegger, but Arnold Schwarzenegger worked on himself physically for more than twenty years to develop a prize-winning physique.

You have the same mental muscles as anyone else. Your job is to work on your mental muscles and build yourself up so that you have a prize-winning mental physique in the areas for which you are best suited so that you can accomplish the goals that are most important to you. Your intelligence is malleable over a range of about twenty-five points. This means that no matter how smart you are, you can be vastly smarter by simply going to work and pumping mental iron to build up your mental muscles.

With a concentrated physical fitness program, you can become superbly fit physically; with a concentrated mental development program, you can become superbly fit mentally as well. You can become one of the smartest and most competent and capable people in your field by working on your mental muscles in the ways that I will talk about below.

The most important single quality for success in your life and relationships is optimism. Optimism can be defined in several ways. First of all, it is a positive and constructive approach towards yourself and your life. The optimist accepts that life is challenging, but sees far more possibilities and opportunities than obstacles and difficulties. Optimists are extremely solution-oriented. Whenever faced with a problem of any kind, they stop and ask, what is the solution? What do we do now? What's the next step? Optimists are so busy working on solutions that they have no time to sit around worrying about the problems.

Optimists are also extremely future-oriented. They think in terms of the next step: What do we do now? Where are we going, and how are we going to get there? They look for the good in every person and situation. They look for the valuable lesson in every setback or difficulty. They are always seeking a way to benefit from the inevitable challenges and tests that life throws up.

Above all, optimists are always asking *how*. This should be your operational question as well. Whenever you think of something that you want to be or have or do, your first question should be, *how?* The more you ask this question, the less time and energy you'll spend on reasons why success may not be possible for you.

The better thinking tools you have, the more positive and optimistic you become; the higher your integrative intelligence becomes. The more thinking tools you have, the easier it is for you to develop solutions and possibilities that will help you to move ahead faster and further than anyone else in attaining your goal. The better you think, the more rapidly you will break through the conscious and unconscious success barriers that may have been holding you back. The better and more effectively you think, the more confident, positive, and optimistic you'll become.

Nothing succeeds like success. The more successful you are in attaining your goals, the happier and more confident you become; consequently the more you like and respect yourself, so you set higher and better goals for yourself. The higher and better goals you set for yourself, the more you accomplish, and the more you like and respect yourself, you put yourself onto an upward spiral that leads to ever higher levels of success and achievement.

One of the most important insights you'll ever learn is this: whatever problem you have has already been solved by someone else. Whatever goal you have has already been achieved by hundreds and perhaps thousands and even millions of other people already. You do not have to reinvent the wheel. You simply have to find out how others have achieved the same goal. You need to find the solution that successful people have discovered and used effectively and use it yourself. Then you do the same things, and you'll get the same results.

Many people are succeeding greatly today partly because many people have succeeded greatly before them. The smartest people are out gathering the combined wisdom and knowledge of successful people who have gone before them and then applying it to their lives, work, and families. When you start to practice the ideas that I will present in this book, you'll begin to move ahead further and faster than perhaps you ever imagined before.

Throughout history, going back to Thucydides and his history of the Peloponnesian War in the fifth century BC, the thinking styles and behaviors of the greatest military leaders of all times have been studied exhaustively. These methods of thinking—or principles of military strategy, as they're called—are now taught in military colleges and schools worldwide. Leading commanders have used twelve principles of strategic thinking to achieve great military successes in turbulent and chaotic situations, often against overwhelming odds and with tremendous disadvantages.

As a student of military history, I've always been fascinated by the parallels between the principles of military strategy and those of business success. The more I studied these parallels, the more I realized that they're the same principles that account for success in personal life as well.

Ways of thinking and acting that have proven effective by the most successful leaders of history in the most difficult situations can be very helpful in giving us direction and insights on handling our inevitable daily challenges. Military leaders usually had to achieve victory against determined enemies, usually far from home, while often vastly outnumbered, with the fate of armies, empires, nations, and even civilizations at stake.

Your goals—and mine—are much simpler: we want to be healthy and happy, have good relationships, be successful in our work, and achieve financial independence. From our own point of view, these goals are as important, if not more important, to us than the goals of military leaders at critical points in history.

The principles that I will outline in this book—the thinking tools and keys to breaking your success barriers and achieving your goals faster and more easily than ever before—are derived from military strategy, but you can use them in every area of your life.

For the purposes of this book, I have chosen to call these principles the *warrior mindset*. You can add them to your mental toolbox to solve your problems more easily, overcome your obstacles more effectively, and achieve your goals more rapidly than you could without them, and more rapidly than anyone else around you.

There are virtually no limits on what you can have, be, and do when you break through your mental success barriers by using the critical thinking principles that I'll discuss.

1

The Principle of the Objective

The first principle is the principle of the *objective*. In military terms, the principle of the objective comes before all else. Fuzziness with regard to objectives is the primary reason for failure, frustration, and underachievement in every area, including warfare, business, and personal goals. Conversely, clarity about objectives is the most important factor in success. When U.S. chief of staff George C. Marshall sent Dwight D. Eisenhower to Europe to coordinate the Allied forces in World War II, his objective was simple: proceed to London, invade Europe, and defeat the Germans. When General Norman Schwarzkopf was sent to the Persian Gulf in 1990, his objective was simple as well: to get the Iraqi army out of Kuwait.

In business, the ability to set clear goals and objectives for every area and for every person in every department is the first prerequisite for success and profitability. On the other hand, uncertainty about goals and objectives is the primary cause of the wasted time and money, demoralization, unhappiness. and lack of direction that plague so many businesses today.

For you personally, the principle of the objective means setting clear, specific goals for every part of your life. Your ability to set goals and make plans for their accomplishment is the master skill of success. With clear goals, you can accomplish almost anything, but without goals, you must always work for someone else who has goals of their own.

You need goals for your personal life. You need goals for your family life. You need goals for your business and your career. You need personal and professional development goals. You need spiritual goals and goals for inner development, and you need community goals that have to do with the contribution you want to make to your society.

Decide today to make the coming year the very best year of your life. Resolve today that no matter what has happened in the past, that was then, and this is now. Begin your goal setting process by imagining that you have no limitations whatsoever on what you can be, have, and do.

Imagine that you have all the time and money, all the people and contacts, all the knowledge and skill, and all the resources that you need to achieve anything you want. Imagine that you've just won $1 million cash, and you have it in the bank. Imagine that you are guaranteed success in any goal you set for yourself. Always start your process of goal setting as if you had no limitations at all and you were starting with a clean sheet of paper to design a wonderful life for yourself.

> ## The Steps of Effective Goal Setting
> 1. Decide exactly what you want.
> 2. Write down your goals in order of importance.
> 3. Set a deadline.
> 4. Make a list of everything you will have to do to achieve the goal.
> 5. Organize your goals by time and priority.
> 6. Take action on your plan.
> 7. Do something every day that moves you toward your most important goal.

The Process of Goal Setting

There's a very simple process of goal setting that you can use. There are far more detailed goal setting exercises, all of which are extremely helpful, but here is where you start first: decide exactly what you want. Resist the temptation to be fuzzy or vague. For example, if you want to earn more money, decide upon a specific amount you want to earn within a specific period of time. If you want to enjoy a certain level of health or weight, be specific and clear about what it would be and how you would measure it. Focus and clarity are essential to unlocking the incredible powers of your subconscious mind in attaining the goals that are important to you.

Second, write down your goals. Only 3 percent of adults have written goals, and they accomplish more than everyone else put together. A goal that is not in writing is merely a wish, which is like cigarette smoke in the air: it has no substance or power, nothing that you can get hold of.

So write your goal down. Write it clearly, specifically, in detail. The more details you write into your goal, the more rapidly you'll attain it.

Third, set a deadline. A goal without a deadline is another exercise in wishing and hoping, but when you set a deadline, you create a subconscious forcing system that drives you toward the goal while attracting the goal toward you.

Fourth, make a list of everything you're going to have to do to achieve the goal. The more items you put on your list, the more intensely you begin to believe that the goal is possible for you. The very act of making a list is self-motivational. It creates confidence and courage within you. It makes you more of an optimist. It gives you a sense of power and a feeling of control over your life.

Step number five is to organize your list by time and priority. Make a plan. Decide what you'll have to do first and what you'll have to do later. Second, decide what is more important and what is less important. Especially decide on what is the most important thing that you can do to move you ahead the fastest towards your goal, and start in on that.

Step number six is to take action on your plan. All successful people are intensely action-oriented. Do something immediately. Do it now. Get on with it. Action orientation is the most common single quality of all successful people. Get going, get busy, move fast, develop a sense of urgency, develop a compulsion to closure, a bias for action. Fast tempo is essential to success. All strategic planning is aimed at action *now*. All decision-making must evolve into action *now*. All thinking, hoping, dreaming, and goal setting must be translated into action *now*. Action is everything. You express who you are and what you are in no other way.

Step number seven is to do something every day that moves you toward your most important goal. Once you get into motion in the direction of your dreams, refuse to stop. Resist the temptation to slow down or hesitate. Do something every day to keep the plate spinning, to keep the blood flowing, to keep the momentum moving forward.

One of the best exercises in goal setting I have ever found is to take a blank sheet of paper, write the word *goals* at the top of the page, and write down today's date. Then write down ten goals that you would like to attain in the next twelve months.

Write these goals in the present tense, as if you have already achieved them. For example, if you want to increase your income, you would begin by writing the words, "I earn X number of dollars." If you want to reduce your weight, you would write, "I weigh X number of pounds," as if you had already accomplished it.

Write down at least ten goals. You can write down more if you like, but be sure to write down at least ten. This very act will change your future. If you just put this list away and did not read it for an entire year, when you took it out and read it in twelve months, you would be astonished. One year from today, you would find that 80 percent of your goals have been attained in the most remarkable ways.

If you could only accomplish one goal on your list, which one goal would it be? Once you've decided that, then decide what your second most important goal would be, and then your third, and so on.

Take your most important goal and put it at the top of a clean sheet of paper. Ask yourself, what additional knowledge and skills will I need to attain this goal? Whatever got you to where you are today is not enough to keep you there. To achieve something that you've never achieved before, you're going to have to become someone you've never been before. To attain a goal that is currently beyond anything you have ever attained, you will always have to develop some new quality, attribute, or skill. What is it? What obstacles or difficulties will you have to overcome? What limiting step or constraint sets the speed at which you achieve your goal? Is it something in yourself, or something in the situation around you?

In military terms, the principle of the objective requires directing all efforts toward a clearly defined decisive and obtainable goal. You continually evaluate and reevaluate your plan to make sure that your primary objective is still the most important one that you can attain.

Four Qualities of Leadership

1. Vision
2. Courage
3. Realism
4. Responsibility

Fundamental Qualities of Leadership

The four fundamental qualities of leadership as they apply to goals, objectives, and everything else that I will discuss below are *vision, courage, realism,* and *responsibility.*

Vision means having a clear mental picture of what you want to accomplish and where you want to end up. All leaders have vision. They can see the big picture. They have an exciting image or idea of the ideal future for themselves, their family, their companies, and their customers. What is your vision? What are you trying to accomplish or attain? What will it look like when you achieve it?

The second quality of leadership is *courage*: having the inner strength to do whatever it takes to achieve the vision. You have the self-discipline and willpower to practice your highest values. You have the willingness to go forward to initiate action with no guarantee of success. Courage is a foundational quality of all great success.

The third quality of leadership is *realism* or intellectual honesty: the ability and willingness to deal with the world as it is rather than as you wish it were. You are honest about your strengths and weaknesses and those of your company and your situation. You don't fool yourself or practice self-delusion. You are perfectly honest and objective about who you are, what you want accomplish, and what you will have to do to get from here to there.

The fourth quality of leadership is *responsibility*: accepting that you are where you are and what you are because of yourself. You refuse to make excuses or blame anyone else. You refuse to complain or criticize. You say, "If it's to be, it's up to me."

Leaders think about the future: they project forward one, two, three, four, and five years. Where do you want to be in five years? If everything works out perfectly for you, what will it look like? Remember, this is the best time in all of human history to be alive. There have never been more opportunities and possibilities for you than exist today, and the only real limits on what you can do, have, and be, are those that you impose on your own thinking—either because of your own doubts and fears or because you are not yet applying the thinking skills practiced by the most successful men and women in history.

As soon as you can, take a blank sheet of paper, write out your ten goals, organize them by priority, select the most important goal, and make a plan for its attainment. Then every day do something specific and tangible that moves you at least one step closer to your goal. When you begin to implement the principle of the objective into every part of your life and begin to work from clear, specific written goals, you'll be on your way to breaking the success barrier.

In the next chapter, we'll talk about the second principle of military strategy: the principle of the *offensive*. We will talk about how important it is to decide upon specific actions and carry them out.

Key Points

- Success is the direct consequence of your thinking.
- You can change the way you are by changing your thinking.
- When you think and act the way successful people do, you will become successful.
- You have no control over challenges that may arise. You can only control your response to them.
- The greatest barriers to success are fear and doubt.
- Optimism is a key factor for success.
- Optimists are always asking *how*.
- Your effectiveness depends on your ability to integrate information.
- The more successful you are in attaining your goals, the happier and more confident you become.

2

The Offensive

The second principle of war is the principle of the *offensive*. This is simple: seize, retain, and exploit the initiative. In adhering to this principle, the commander sets the pace, determines the course of battle, exploits enemy weaknesses, and capitalizes on unexpected developments.

Robert Ronstadt, former vice president of Boston University, called this the *corridor principle.* He found that successful entrepreneurs launch themselves in the direction of their goals, entering into a corridor of possibilities and opportunities. As they move down the corridor, other doors, other opportunities appear to the right and left that lead them into areas that they had not originally anticipated.

Most success comes in areas different from where you thought it would be. The famed World War II general George S. Patton Jr. once said that in war the only sure defense is offense, and the efficiency of the offense depends on the warlike souls of those conducting it.

The principle of the offensive applies at all levels of the company—strategic, operational, and tactical. No company will survive in a highly competitive environment if management hesitates to take the risks involved in seizing the initiative. No matter what the business, retaining the initiative of offensive action forces the competitors to react rather than to proact.

Offensive action in the marketplace is vital to achieving decisive results and maintaining freedom of action. It permits the manager to exercise initiative and impose his or her will on the competitor. Napoleon once said that no great battles are ever won on the defensive.

Psychologists have determined that the foundation of a positive mental attitude, a feeling of optimism, arises from a sense of control. You have a sense of control when you feel that you are in control of your own life. You feel out of control when you feel that your life is controlled by someone or something else.

Most stress arises from a feeling that important parts of your life or work are controlled by others. In fact, if you want to become your own psychologist, look around your life at the areas that are causing you stress and define exactly why and how you feel other people or circumstances are controlling you. High-performance men and women have a very high personal sense of control. They see themselves as the primary creative forces in their own lives. They see themselves as in charge of themselves and whatever happens to them.

Ineffective people—people subject to negative emotions, excuses, and blaming—invariably feel out of control. They feel that they are controlled by their circumstances—their bills, their bosses, their families. As a result, they complain and criticize on a regular basis without realizing that they are actually in charge.

Action orientation gives you a tremendous sense of control. When you are taking specific actions in the direction of specific goals that you have set for yourself, you feel powerful rather than powerless; you feel like a master of change. You feel you are making things happen rather than waiting for them to happen. In times of turbulence and rapid change, you are far better off taking continual action in the direction of your goals and objectives than by playing it safe.

A sense of forward momentum is essential for happiness and well-being. It's been said that happiness is the progressive realization of a worthy ideal. What does this mean? When you feel that you are moving step by step toward the accomplishment of something that is important to you, you feel very much in control of your life; as you make progress, even in very small increments, you feel more and more like a winner. Your self-esteem and self-respect go up. You feel stronger and more confident. You develop higher levels of courage and persistence. You feel unstoppable. On the other hand, when you slow down or stop, you start to feel negative and demotivated. Your morale declines. You're more susceptible to negative influences.

This is why all successful people seem to be in continual motion. They are busy all the time. They are moving all day long. The faster you move, the more ground you cover; the faster you move, the more people you see and the better results you get. The faster you move, the more energy you have and the more enthusiastic you are, and the more successful and respected you are by everyone around you.

Learn from the Mongols

Continual action is indispensable to your happiness, success, and high achievement, and it is very much a decision that you make. It is perhaps the best success strategy of all. You are constantly in motion. You become a moving target. You are impossible to nail down. Nobody can take you for granted. If you're not trying one thing, you're trying something else. If one thing doesn't work for you, you've already started on two or three other things. As a result, you put the law of probabilities on your side. You dramatically increase your likelihood of success, because you are trying far more and different things than the average person.

One of the largest empires in world history was the Mongol Empire of the Middle Ages. At its height, the Mongol Empire dominated the territory from the Sea of Japan to the Danube in Europe, including much of China, India, most of Russia, and almost all of the Middle East to the Mediterranean. If it had not been for the death of its great leader, Genghis Khan, and the recall of the Mongol armies from the Danube, they might have swept across all of Europe. However, the Mongols were always vastly outnumbered. Each Mongol army consisted of 20,000 armed cavalry, but because they were so fast on the offensive, because they moved so quickly and used deception so well, they were able to encircle and defeat vastly superior forces time after time.

The losers from these conflicts went home and talked about the Mongol horde as if it were made up of millions of soldiers. The Mongol armies were never very large (even today, the population of Mongolia is fairly small), but they were brilliant at offensive action. They were able to move so quickly and take advantage of every opportunity far faster than their opponents that they were able to conquer most of the known world.

One tactic was called the Mongol siege. This principle has direct application to your life and work today. The Mongol army would approach a walled city. They would send emissaries to arrange a truce and a surrender. If the city refused to surrender, the Mongols would surround it and cut off all supplies going in and out. They would then initiate a series of probes against the walls of the city in different places. Once they had found a place along the wall where a breakthrough was likely, the army would divide into three shifts. They would begin the attack. One shift, consisting of one third of the army, would attack at that section of the wall until it was relieved by the next shift, and then by the next. The siege would go on for twenty-four hours a day until the wall fell. Once the wall fell, the city would quickly be overrun and fall into Mongol hands. The Mongol army would then proceed on to the next city.

The principle of the Mongol siege applies to your life as well. The attitude of continual sustained attack toward the achievement of any goal will do more to guarantee your ultimate success than any other decision you can make.

People underachieve and fail in life not because of lack of ability and opportunity, but because they lack focus and a continual offensive strategy. They may start strong, but they soon quit and back off and relax. They take it easy. They approach life and work casually, and as the late inspirational speaker Jim Rohn said, casualness in business causes casualties.

The key to the continual offensive is courage. As the great British author C. S. Lewis once wrote, courage is not simply one of the virtues, but the form of every virtue at the testing point. The good news is that the clearer you are about your objectives and the more thoroughly you plan your offensive, the more courage and willingness you will have to act and the more persistent you will in sustaining the action until you achieve the result you desire.

The major reason for failure is not failure itself, but the fear of failure. Everyone fails far more than they succeed. Charles Kettering, the noted research scientist at General Electric, once said that an inventor fails 999 times, but if he succeeds once, he is in. He treats his failures simply as practice shots.

Phil Knight, founder of Nike, said that the most valuable lesson he ever learned came from a business professor who said, "You only have to succeed the last time. You can fail countless times, but one great success wipes away all your failures." Many writers will write books and submit them year after year, accumulating hundreds and even thousands of rejection slips from publishers, but then one book will be accepted and become a best seller. Forever after, the writer will be a hero or heroine. All the years of frustration and failure are wiped away by one great success.

In Operation Desert Storm during the Gulf War, the command spent six solid months in planning and preparation before launching the aerial bombardment. After thirty days of bombardment, they stopped and asked the Iraqis if they would like to surrender and withdraw from Kuwait. When the Iraqis spurned the offer, the United States and its allies launched the ground attack, which of course had been in preparation for months. When it was launched, 330,000 allied soldiers slashed across the desert like a sword and cut off the entire Iraqi army at Basra, bringing the war to a swift conclusion in just 100 hours. But after all the aerial bombardment, in the final analysis it was the willingness and the ability of the allied forces to take the offensive that settled the issue.

In business, companies that spend more on research and development, constantly upgrading and improving their products and services, are vastly more successful over time than those that continue to sell a successful product or service without innovations or improvements. There seems to be a direct relationship between the percentage of sales that is committed to ongoing research and development and to the long-term growth and profitability of the company. Business researchers have found that the most successful companies have a higher rate of new product introduction than the less successful companies. Companies like Rubbermaid, for example, introduce a new product every single day. These products are developed in conjunction and consultation with their customers and their customers' specific needs.

Most successful companies aim to have 80 percent of their sales in any given year coming from products that have been developed in the last five years. Of course, the failure rate on new product introductions is about 80 percent. In any given year, thousands of new products and services will be brought to the market. Fully 80 percent will fail, even after the most exhaustive market research and testing. Of the 20 percent that succeed, about 75 percent of those will be reasonably profitable, and perhaps one out of twenty will be a big hit.

Every effort is made to improve these odds, but in times of rapid growth of knowledge, information, technology, and increasing competition, these odds seem to hold true over time. Consequently, individuals and companies that want to be successful in our competitive marketplace have to play the game by the new rules—and the new rules are that you must be on the continual offensive. You must be continually advancing, moving forward, trying new things, introducing new products and services, and new ways of selling and marketing those products and services.

If you're in sales and you want to make the next twelve months the best twelve months of your life and double your income, here's a simple technique that seems to work for everybody anywhere. Just decide today that you are going to call on 100 new prospects as fast as you can. Don't worry about whether or not you make any sales. Develop a very simple introduction and sales presentation. Don't play games. Introduce yourself. Tell them what you're selling, and ask them if they're interested. If not, ask them why not. If they are, immediately give them the information they need to help them to make a buying decision. But the most important thing is that you don't worry whether or not any one of these contacts turns into a sale. Your attitude of wanting the business, but not too much, will relax both you and the customer. It'll enable you to learn about your business and its strengths and weaknesses faster than you can imagine. More than anything else, this attitude will enable you to make calls and open doors that you may have been reluctant to approach if you are preoccupied with making a sale.

In business, the one thing we know is that whatever business strategy you are currently using, it'll stop working sooner or later. Whatever form of advertising or promotion you are using, if it's successful, will soon be copied by your competitors. You have to keep asking yourself, what is my next miracle going to be?

The GOSPA Formula

You must be continually putting yourself on the offensive, continually seeking for new ways to take the initiative and take control of your forward momentum.

There's a simple formula that you can use to become more effective on the offensive. It is called the GOSPA formula, and it is used for strategic planning at both the highest levels of business and at the simplest levels of personal success. The five letters stand for *goals, objectives, strategies, plans,* and *actions.* Let's take them one at a time.

> **The GOSPA Formula**
>
> **G**oals **O**bjectives **S**trategies **P**lans **A**ctions

Goals are the final end states or results that you plan to attain. A goal is a destination. It is clear, specific, and time-bounded. Once it is attained, you can go on to the next goal. As I mentioned in the previous chapter, your ability to be perfectly clear about exactly what you want and what it will look like when you attain it is essential to unlocking your mental powers.

For example, a good goal is to double your income within the next two or three years. Doubling your income will probably do more to help you achieve more of your other goals than the attainment of any other aim. In any event, clarity and specificity with regard to your goal is the starting point.

The second letter, O, stands for *objectives*. These are the things that you will have to do, the steps that you'll have to take in order to attain your goal. There may be one, or there may be several. For example, if you want to double the sales or double the income of your entire company, there are a series of objectives that must first be achieved. If you want to double your personal sales and your personal income, there are several objectives as well. To double your sales, for example, you're going to have to either double the number of people you sell to or double the amount you sell to each person or a combination of the two.

Another objective, which actually comes before, may be to double your skills and abilities in a particular area. In sales, this might include prospecting, presenting, or getting referrals. What objectives will you have to attain in order to achieve your goals, such as doubling your income?

Whatever they are, write them down. Organize them by importance: which are more important and which are less important? Organize them by priority: which need to be accomplished immediately, and which can be accomplished later? These steps need to be covered even in planning a military offensive.

The next letter in the GOSPA formula, S, stands for *strategies*. These are the different ways by which you can go about attaining the objectives that you must achieve in order to accomplish your goal. For example, a company that wants to double its sales may decide to double the size of its sales force. That is one strategy. Another company may decide to train its people more intensively and double their sales skills and abilities. That's another strategy. Still another company may decide to outsource the entire prospecting function to a telemarketing company that specializes in prospecting for this type of product or service. This is a third strategy.

SWOT Analysis

Strengths   Weaknesses   Opportunities   Threats

When you use the GOSPA model, you are continually doing what is called a *SWOT analysis*. SWOT stands for *strengths, weaknesses, opportunities,* and *threats*. What are the strengths and weaknesses of each of your strategies? What are the strengths and weaknesses of each part of your organization relative to a particular strategy?

What are the opportunities in the marketplace and what are the threats represented by changes or by competition?

Here are two of the major mistakes made by business people today. One is, "I want to, therefore I can." Many people confuse desire and ability. Just because you want to do something doesn't mean that you are capable of it. Many companies that try to get into different businesses or industries end up losing enormous amounts of money because they find that they simply do not have the ability to be in that particular industry. You have to be perfectly honest with yourself in deciding whether or not you have the ability to carry out a strategy before you embark upon it. Just because you *want to* doesn't mean that you *can*.

A second, similar mistake is thinking that, "Because I need to, I can." Just because you need to survive and thrive doesn't mean that you are able to. You must be very honest in this area, or you can cause yourself tremendous difficulties. What are your strengths? What are your opportunities? What are your unique capabilities? What can you definitely do if you decide to do it? Be perfectly and unflinchingly honest and objective about your abilities and your situation. Jack Welch, the famed CEO of General Electric, once said, "We will be first or second in every market we go into, or we will leave that market." He went on to say, "If you don't have competitive advantage, don't compete." In short, if you unable to do something with excellence, you should not commit resources to doing it in a halfway fashion. Some of the smartest individuals and organizations deliberately decide to abandon a particular industry or market in order to focus on an area where they have the ability to achieve leadership.

The fourth letter in the GOSPA model, P, stands for *plans*. Once you have clear goals, have established the objectives necessary to achieve them and selected the strategies you are going to use, you plan out each strategy. The 20/80 rule applies to planning: the 20 percent of the time that you spend planning and thinking about what you're going to do before you take the offensive will be worth 80 percent of the value of your eventual results.

Plans are fairly simple to organize. Simply brainstorm a list of every single thing you can possibly do to carry out the strategy. Write it all down, review the list after a day, and add to it. Keep adding to your list until you can think of nothing else that you can possibly do to carry out the strategy. Then organize the list in terms of importance and priorities. What comes first and what comes second? What is more important, and what is less important?

The last letter in the GOSPA model, A, stands for *actions*: the specific activities you will engage in to carry out the plan, fulfill the strategy, achieve the objective, and obtain the goal. Actions are specific, measurable, time-bounded, and assigned to particular individuals. *Someone* is responsible. Nothing is left a chance. Everybody knows exactly what they're supposed to do, when and how they're supposed to do it, and how it'll be measured. Everybody knows what everyone else is supposed to do as well.

The time you take to think through and plan the attainment of your major goal will yield rewards out of all proportion to the effort. Even though the plan will change as soon as it is launched, the very act of thinking through all the details will assure a far higher probability of success than if you had launched before considering everything that could possibly go wrong. Successful people do not necessarily make the right decisions every time, but they make their decisions right. One advantage of a continual action philosophy, of being on the offensive all the time, is that you get more and faster feedback than any other way.

After convertibles had been out of fashion for some years, Lee Iacocca, then president of Chrysler, wanted to find out if there was a market for a new Chrysler convertible. He asked his engineers how long it would take them to get him a convertible that he could drive around in. They told him that it would take about two years. He explained to them that he wanted it immediately. They could take a blowtorch and remove the top of an existing car, and that would be fine for him.

Iacocca then took his new convertible and drove it through the streets of Detroit. Everywhere he went, people waved at him and smiled. That was all the market research he needed. He went back to the plant and ordered them to produce a convertible, which became a tremendous market success.

Peak performers are famous for rapid action. They then get immediate feedback and self-correct. When they acquire a piece of information that contradicts their previous ideas, they immediately incorporate it into their existing information base and change it if necessary. They are moving targets. They seldom stop for any period of time.

Managers who practice the principle of the offensive are in continual motion as well. They are moving and intermingling with their staff on a regular basis. They are out among them, getting their questions, ideas, problems, and feedback moment by moment. They always know what is going on, because they always have their hands on the pulse of the business.

The most successful sales managers spend 70 percent or more of their time in the field with their salespeople, calling on customers. As a result, they're very aware of what their salespeople are facing, what customers are asking for, and what questions or problems exist in the marketplace that the company needs to change or correct.

During World War II, the German general Erwin Rommel was known as the Desert Fox. He was one of the best generals of the twentieth century. His strategy was continual action, continual offensive. When he was sent by Hitler to North Africa to support the Italians against the British, the British knew he was coming but weren't worried. They assumed that it would take him several weeks to unload his troops, tanks, and munitions and begin moving toward the front, but that was not Rommel's style at all. As his men, tanks, and trucks came off the ships at Tripoli, he immediately launched an attack on the British positions. As more men and tanks came off the ships, they were rushed forward. This caught the British totally by surprise. They lost almost their entire armored division in the desert and fled back to Egypt. Although he was always outnumbered, Rommel's, unrelenting, continual offenses disconcerted the British at every turn.

Perhaps the most important part of the principle of the offensive has to do with projecting forward three to five years and deciding where you want to be and what you want to be doing.

What steps will you have to take in order to achieve your goals and objectives three to five years down the road? If you own your own business, you must determine where you want your company to be and how you want it to be known three to five years from now. How do you want people to talk about you in the marketplace? What size company do you want to have, and what kind of reputation do you want to earn? What kind of people do you want working for your company? Whom do you want as your clients? What kind of people will you need to hire and retain? What kind of sales and profit levels will you require to achieve your long-term strategic objectives?

As an individual, you must see yourself as self-employed. You must see yourself as the president of your own company. You must see yourself as the head of an entrepreneurial company with one employee: yourself. You have one product to sell in the marketplace: your services. Your job is to sell the greatest quality and quantity of your services in an ever more competitive marketplace.

What do you have to do to achieve your goals today? What skills and abilities will you have to develop? What steps will you have to take to achieve your goals and objectives in the months and years ahead? As strategic planner Michael Camy once said, those who do not plan for the future cannot have one. The ability to set and achieve strategic objectives is the key skill and the ultimate test of leadership. Leadership is action, not position. Leadership is performance, not planning. Leadership is results more than anything else.

Your ability to think through what you want to accomplish and then act continually in the direction of your goals and dreams is the key to your success. No great battles are ever won on the defensive.

Lessons from Alexander the Great

In 333 BC, at the battle of Issus in modern-day Turkey, the armies of Alexander the Great of Macedon met the armies of King Darius III of Persia in a major conflict. Darius had lined up his armies on one side of the river along the riverbank. While Alexander approached the scene of the battle from the other side of the river, Darius had his forces stretched out for about a quarter of a mile along the riverbank, with his heavy infantry massed in the center of the army and cavalry on the flanks. He expected Alexander to approach on the other side of the river and then arrange his army for battle. Alexander would have to cross the river and attack up the bank, which Darius realized would put Alexander at an extreme disadvantage.

The two generals had never met in battle before. However, Alexander had tremendous courage. He was never known to be afraid of anything. He also had the ability to move so fast that no one around him ever got a chance to think about being afraid themselves. Alexander sent scouts forward who came back and reported on the deployment of Persian troops. Alexander then sent messengers up and down the army as he led them forward. When they arrived at the scene of the battle, instead of stopping and organizing his forces, Alexander's cavalry, with himself at the lead, attacked off the march. The Persian forces arrayed along the far bank were standing around, some of them eating lunch, watching the opposing troops come up. Suddenly, Alexander and his 6,000 Macedonian cavalrymen attacked across the river and struck right into the center of the Persian army.

Alexander always believed that the enemy was the weakest at its strongest point: he felt that whatever the enemy was protecting the most heavily was where he could achieve the greatest psychological advantage by striking first. The Persian army was arrayed around the person of Darius the king, and this is where Alexander attacked. The Persian army was taken by complete surprise. Meanwhile, the Macedonian cavalry at the end of the army had crossed the river and were sweeping down the bank on the left flank of the Persians. Suddenly, from a relatively calm day, there were Macedonians, not only in the center of the Persian army, but attacking from the outside as well. The Persian army broke up in complete disarray and confusion. Even though the Persian army numbered more than 50,000 troops and Alexander's army was just over 22,000 men and cavalry, the Persians were completely defeated in less than two hours.

Author Dorothea Brande once wrote these wonderful words about courage and success: "Decide exactly what you want, and then act as if it were impossible to fail." Your desire, your aim, your goal is to be a big success. Decide exactly what your goal is and sit down and make a plan to attain it. Then take action and continue taking action relentlessly until you overcome all obstacles and eventually win through.

Action orientation is and always has been the most obvious and observable quality of all successful people, and you can develop it if you decide to. Nothing can stop you but yourself, and there's no better or faster way for you to break through the success barrier than by attacking it head on. As Michael Jordan says, "Just do it."

Key Points

- The principle of the offensive: seize, retain, and exploit the initiative.
- A positive mental attitude arises from a sense of control.
- Ineffective people feel out of control.
- Successful people are in continual motion.
- Casualness in business causes casualties.
- Courage is the form of every virtue at the testing point.
- You only have to succeed the last time.
- The GOSPA formula: goals, objectives, strategies, plans, and actions.
- Project forward three to five years to decide where you want to be and what you want to be doing.
- See yourself as the president of your own company.
- Decide exactly what you want, and then act as if it were impossible to fail.

3

Simplify!

We are living in the busiest time in all of human history. You have too much to do and too little time in which to do it, and the rate of change and complexity in your life is probably increasing every single day. To break through your success barriers and accomplish everything that you are capable of, you must learn how to simplify your life.

In military strategy, the principle of simplicity is defined in this way: prepare clear, uncomplicated plans and clear, concise orders to ensure thorough understanding. In all communications, the commander should make every reasonable effort to eliminate the slightest chance of misunderstanding. Simplicity contributes to this end.

In your life, the principle of simplicity means continually looking for ways to reduce the number of things you are doing so that you can concentrate your time, attention, and energies on those things that will make the greatest contribution to your life and your goals.

Throughout most of human history, land was the primary source of value. Most wars were fought over the possession of land and property. Empires grew in proportion to their ability to seize and control land. Because most of the world was agricultural, it was believed that possession of the agricultural basis of a society was the key to acquiring and keeping wealth and power.

At the beginning of the twentieth century, the emphasis shifted to capital. Throughout that century, most of the major conflicts were over the acquisition of capital: factories, machinery, buildings, equipment, and cities. Money and the things that money could buy were the driving force of human activity.

Now, however, we are going through a major paradigm shift. Land and capital are still important, but the primary source of value is knowledge. Your ability to acquire practical, usable knowledge and quickly apply it to benefit others is the key to your financial future and success. The principle of simplicity is essential to determining how you can do more of the things that contribute the highest value to the world around you.

The most important principle in personal effectiveness is the principle of clarity, combined with the principle of concentration (which I'll talk about below). Your goal is to develop a keen sense for the things that you can do that contribute real value to the world around you, and then to concentrate on those things. You must discipline yourself to avoid distractions and diversions into areas that may be fun and easy, but which contribute very little. Side roads are slide roads.

Throughout human history, all progress has come about as the result of simplification in science, technology, manufacturing, business, medicine, and every other area of human endeavor. Simplification means that with new and better ways of thinking and acting, it takes less time and expense to accomplish the same or greater results. Your job is to organize your life so that you are doing fewer things, but things of greater importance and value.

How do you decide whether something is important? Simple: you review your goals and aims. Every activity can be weighed, measured, and evaluated in terms of what you really want out of your life, your relationships, and your work. Anything that contributes toward the achievement of your goals is a good and valuable use of time. Anything that does not contribute to that end is not a good use of time. Moreover, the greater the potential contribution of a particular activity to the achievement of your goals, the higher value that activity has. Everything else is a relative waste of time.

The principle of simplicity requires that you continually look for ways to reduce the number of steps and the amount of time that it takes you to accomplish a particular task. Time is money. Time is life. Time is both perishable and irreplaceable. It cannot be saved; it can only be spent. It can only be reallocated away from activities of lower value toward those of higher value. The more activities of higher value you can do, the better, happier, and more prosperous life you are going to have. Simplifying your life can dramatically improve the quality of your activities and your results.

The Law of Complexity

Some years ago, after studying the differences between simplicity and complexity for a long time, I came up with what I call *the law of complexity*. The law of complexity says that the number of steps in any process has an inordinate effect on the time, complexity, and potential cost of that process. My formula is that the potential cost, the potential number of mistakes, and the potential time required for any activity increases by the square of the number of steps that it takes to complete that activity. Let me explain.

> **The law of complexity: the number of steps in any process has an inordinate effect on the time, complexity, and potential cost of that process.**

For example, if you decide to make a phone call to give a message to someone, that is a one-step activity. The square of one is still one. The level of complexity is very low. The likelihood of lost time and expenditure is very low as well. There is very little room for misunderstanding or miscommunication.

However, let us say that you ask someone else to make a telephone call for you and pass on a message. Now you have two steps to the process. The level of complexity is two squared, or a level of four. The person may or may not make the call and may or may not pass on the message accurately. The person receiving the message may not understand exactly what you want to accomplish with the call. The complexity goes up from a factor of one when you make the call yourself to a complexity factor of four when you have someone else make the call.

This is perhaps why many senior executives place their own calls and answer their own phones. They realize that even though it seems a bit inconvenient, it can save an enormous amount of time and misunderstanding in the long run.

Now let us suppose that you ask someone else *to ask someone else* to make a call to pass along a message and get a piece of information. You now have three steps in the process. Three squared is nine, or a complexity level of nine. The likelihood of a mistake or miscommunication and a need to make a follow-up telephone call to clarify or rectify the situation is nine times greater than if you had simply called yourself.

Before I developed this law of complexity, I would involve a lot of people in even the simplest projects in my company. At one point, we decided to put out a newsletter announcing some of our new products to our distributors. Six people were involved. The items to be decided were the copy or written material, the paper stock, the artwork or layout, the mailing lists, and the mailing house that would handle it. There were also colors to be used in the printing, the printer to be used, the cost and scheduling of the printer, the products to be mentioned, and the different price points of the products, as well as several other factors.

Each person was going to be responsible for one or more of the activities that had to be carried out to produce and mail the newsletter. With six people involved, we already had a complexity level of six squared, or thirty-six. Since each of these people had one or more responsibilities, the complexity level was completely out of sight. Instead of getting the newsletter out in a couple of weeks, it was still not out six months later. When the newsletter finally did go out, the color was wrong, the type size was wrong, and there was no return address that people could use to phone or respond. It was a nightmare.

The next time we decided to do a newsletter, one person decided the copy and content, and another person was responsible for artwork, design, and mailing. The newsletter was complete and out the door within thirty days, without mistakes.

Complexity causes an enormous amount of stress and strain. Think of the areas where you feel overwhelmed with too much to do in too little time: you begin to feel like a rat on a treadmill, running faster and faster and making very little progress. Sometimes you can't sleep at night because you are tossing and turning, worrying that you will not be able to get everything done in the time available.

The key is to simplify your life in every way possible. Here are some simplification techniques that are used by the most effective, most productive, and highest-paid people in our society.

The Power of the List

First, think on paper. There's no better or faster way to get your life under control than to take a pad of paper, think of everything you have to do, and begin writing each item down one by one. A pad of paper is the most powerful time management tool that I've ever discovered. The very act of writing down everything that you have to do for the foreseeable future will give you a tremendous sense of control, making you feel you are on top of your activities rather than being overwhelmed by them. And the very act of writing out and organizing a list of activities begins immediately to make you more efficient and effective at everything you do.

In 1918, Charles M. Schwab (not to be confused with the investment advisor Charles R. Schwab) was the manager of the titanic Bethlehem Steel Company. He engaged Ivy Lee, a celebrated management expert, and asked him, "Show me a way to get more things done."

"Give me fifteen minutes with each of your executives," Lee replied.

"How much will it cost me?" asked Schwab.

"Nothing," said Lee. "Unless it works. After three months, you can send me a check for whatever you feel it's worth to you."

Lee met with each executive and taught them this technique:

At the end of each day, each executive was to write down the six most important tasks they had to accomplish the next day and prioritize them in order of importance.

The next day, the executive was to start by concentrating only on the first task. He was to work on that task until it was completed. He was to approach the rest of his list in the same fashion. At the end of the day, he was to transfer any unfinished items to the list for the next day. He was to repeat this process every workday.

Three months later, Schwab sent Ivy Lee a check for $25,000—which is over $509,000 in 2023 dollars.

You can do the same thing. Make a list of everything you have to do before you begin. Consolidate the list of all of your activities into a single place, preferably a single time planner. There are many time planners on the market today. All of them are good if you will use them on a regular basis; the essence of every time planning system is the same. Get a time planner that has a master list and put everything you have to do at any time in the future goes onto this master list. When something new comes up, quickly jot it down. As the Chinese saying goes, the palest ink is stronger than the finest memory.

From your master list, create a monthly list: write down everything that you have to do for that month. As new things come up, either write them down on your master list or add them to your monthly list.

From your monthly list, create a weekly list. Plan every week in advance, preferably the weekend before. I've spoken to many successful people whose lives have turned around completely from confusion and disorder to success and high achievement as the result of taking some time each weekend to plan the coming week in advance, hour by hour.

In fact, you can tell how successful a person is by simply asking them where they will be in two or three days at three o'clock in the afternoon. Successful people know immediately where they will be a few days in the future. Unsuccessful people have no idea.

From your weekly list, you create a daily list. The best time to create a daily list is the night before. This allows your subconscious mind to work on your list throughout the night. When you awaken in the morning, you will often have insights and ideas on accomplishing your goals and completing your activities more efficiently and effectively.

In any event, make a list before you begin. Work on your list throughout the day. Whenever something new comes up—even a telephone call or a request to pass on a message—jot it down on your list. At the end of your day, you can go over your list, and you'll have a clear record of everything you've accomplished. A major source of stress today is the feeling that you've been working hard all day long but have accomplished very little. When you work from a list, you'll not only have a sense of control and personal power, but as you review your list at the end of the day, you'll have a tremendous sense of accomplishment as well.

At the end of each day, take your list and create a new list for the coming day. Transfer all the things that you have been unable to accomplish from one list to the next. When your list is complete, your day is over. You can then relax and forget about it knowing that you are completely organized and ready to go when you get up the next morning.

To simplify your life, set priorities on the activities on your list. Remember the 80/20 rule: 20 percent of the things you do will account for 80 percent of the value of all the things you do. You must always be working on the 20 percent of activities that account for most of the value.

In a recent experiment, a group of managers was asked to list all the things that they enjoyed doing the most at work. These activities were written on a flip chart, and the pages were taped on the wall.

The managers were then asked to list all the things that they found the most difficult or distasteful to do. These items were listed on a separate flip chart and posted on the wall as well. Then the 80/20 rule was introduced and discussed.

The managers were asked which list contained the 80 percent of activities that contributed very little and which list contained the 20 percent that contributed most of the value. Somewhat embarrassed, they admitted that the big, difficult, unpleasant tasks on the second list also happened to be the 20 percent that contributed the greatest value.

It's always the same: fun, easy tasks contribute very little, but big, difficult tasks can often have enormous consequences. The key is contained in the word *consequences*. The potential consequences of an activity determine its likely value or lack of value. Some things that you do during the course of the day have no potential consequences at all.

It's amazing how many people come to work and the first thing they start thinking and talking about is their coffee and lunch breaks. Yet you could take coffee breaks for the next thirty years and they would make no contribution whatsoever to your work or your life. Coffee and lunch breaks have no potential consequences—certainly no positive consequences—for your career.

On the other hand, you can do certain things immediately that can have enormous potential consequences. Some activities will bring about tremendous results that can help you and your organization to move ahead. These activities will almost always be more difficult and challenging than the fun, easy things, but successful people are far more concerned about pleasing results and achievement than they are about pleasing methods and activities.

The ABCDE Method

You can use a simple ABCDE method to organize your list of activities before you begin. This is a tremendous tool for simplification and dramatically increases the quality and quantity of your output.

The method simply requires that you think before you begin. Before beginning, you must be absolutely clear in your own mind about the most valuable uses of your time.

The ABCDE Method

A. Things you must do
B. Activities with mild consequences
C. Activities with no consequences
D. Items to delegate
E. Items to eliminate

Once you have your daily list, you go down it and put a letter—an A, B, C, D, or E—next to each activity. A activities are the things that you must do. They have serious potential consequences if you do or don't do them: they will cause real problems if they are not done correctly and on time. Your musts are the most important things on your list. They are the top 20 percent of activities that contribute most of the value of what you do. If you have more than one A activity, then organize them by A1, A2, A3, and so on.

The second type consists of B activities: activities for which there are merely mild consequences if you do or don't do them. Perhaps someone will be unhappy or inconvenienced, but they are not major consequences. They're not as important as your A tasks. The rule is this: never do a B task when there is an A task left undone.

The third letter, C, stands for activities that have no consequences at all: coffee breaks, lunches, reading papers or newsletters, phoning your family or friends, picking up your dry cleaning, or dropping off your laundry. Whether or not you do them has no potential consequences for your life or career. Again, you must resist doing a C activity when you have B activities left undone, and you must never do a B activity when you have an A activity left undone.

This decision on your part to concentrate on your A activities exclusively is solely a matter of character, willpower, and self-discipline. If you can make yourself concentrate on A activities to the exclusion of all else, you will eventually be a great success. If you cannot, you will always have to work for someone else.

Next is the letter D, which stands for *delegate*: delegate everything you possibly can to anyone else who can do it in order to free up more time for the few things that only you can do. As you develop in your life and career, many activities that you did when you were at a low level of income and responsibility must be delegated to others.

A successful real estate saleswoman once told me that she felt very guilty about not being at home, doing the laundry, preparing the meals, and keeping the house clean for her family.

However, she was so successful in her business that she simply didn't have enough time to do it properly. She felt she was caught on the horns of a dilemma. What could she do?

I explained to her that she was no longer labor; because of her success, she was now a member of management. Her responsibility was not to do the job personally, but to see that the job got done properly by someone else. She had to learn to select and then to delegate. Only then could she satisfy her responsibilities both to her family and to her career.

The same is true for you. You must continually, consciously, and deliberately think about the little things that you do that consume precious minutes and hours that you can delegate to others so that you can free up time to do the things that only you can do.

The fifth letter, E, stands for *eliminate*. This is one of the most important parts of simplifying your life and achieving great success. It has to do with the setting of priorities and the setting of posteriorities. A priority is something that you do more of and sooner. It is an A task that must be done, a task that has serious potential consequences for your life and work. A posteriority, on the other hand, is something that you do less of and later, if at all. A posteriority is something that you discontinue or dramatically reduce the time for accomplishing it.

You must engage in creative abandonment of low-value tasks throughout your lifetime. Many things that you are doing today have little value in comparison with other things that you need to do. When you first began doing them, they may have seemed important or enjoyable, but now, with the passage of time, they are no longer as important as other things that can contribute more to your success.

In order to start something new, you must discontinue something old. Getting in means getting out. Picking up means putting down and setting posteriorities as well as priorities. Simplifying your life by reducing the number of things you are doing is one of the most powerful and essential of all time management principles. You cannot do everything that you have to do. In order to do those few things that really make a difference in your life, you must discontinue doing those things that make a smaller contribution.

If you are unsure about what your posteriorities should be, ask the people around you. Ask them, is there anything that I'm doing that I could discontinue without causing much of a problem? Ask your boss. Ask your coworkers. Ask your secretary. Ask the members of your family. Every one of us has blind spots: activities that we are engaging in, often inefficiently and ineffectively, that make very little contribution to others or ourselves.

We are all creatures of habit. Once we start doing something, we keep on doing it; like Old Man River, we just keep rolling along. Only when we pull ourselves up short or someone else points out that we are spending a lot of time that contributes very little do we suddenly realize that we have gotten into a habit that is not a good use of time.

Once I spoke for a very successful company whose president is a capable and competent businesswoman. After we had discussed the difference between priorities and posteriorities, she told me that she was going to use this idea immediately to dramatically simplify her life. She told me that she was serving on so many boards and committees around her town that she had less and less time for her family and her two young children.

About two weeks later, I got a letter from her. She told me that she had resigned from every community service board and committee except for two. She realized that they only wanted her because she could channel charitable contributions to their organizations. When she assured them that her company would continue making the contributions, she was able to resign from the boards without any complaints. She told me that by simplifying her life, she had dramatically improved the quality of her life in the areas that she considered most important.

You can do the same thing in your own way. What time-consuming activities could you could eliminate, starting immediately? Which activities contribute very little to your life but consume an enormous amount of time?

The average American adult watches five hours and fifteen minutes of television each day. The average American drives around listening to the radio an average of 90 to 120 minutes per day. The average newspaper reader spends anywhere from one to two hours each day reading the newspaper. How many of these activities could you cut back on or eliminate to free up time for far more valuable and important things?

To simplify your life, you can start by getting rid of things. When in doubt, throw it out. We have become a nation of pack rats. We accumulate more and more things, and we try to hold on to them, filling our cupboards, drawers, garages, and even miniwarehouses with things we have not used for months, if not years. We'll probably never use or look at them again, but somehow we cannot bring ourselves to get rid of them. We have an uneasy feeling that sometime, somehow, we might need them again.

Almost everyone in business has piles of reading material that they mean to get to sometime. We keep stacking it up for a later time when we will be caught up with other things and we'll be able to get to it, but somehow we never do. If you haven't read it in the last six months, it is now junk; throw it away. The chances are that you will never need it again. If it is really important, it will soon come out in a different form in a different publication.

Clear your workspace completely. Always work from a clear desk. Avoid the tendency to pile things up. People who say that they can work well in a messy environment have been proved to be wrong. When they're forced to work from a clean desk, they get twice as much done in the same period of time.

Don't allow yourself to justify a messy workspace, a messy desk, a messy briefcase, a messy office, or anything else. You have no idea how much a confused and disorganized working environment can be costing you, both in a feeling of being out of control of your work and in the impression that you are making on other people.

Several management terms have been developed to describe this focus on simplification and increased productivity. I call them the seven R's: *reengineering, reorganization, restructuring, reinventing, reevaluating, refocusing,* and *regaining control.* Let's take each of them one at a time.

The Seven R's

1. Reengineering
2. Reorganization
3. Restructuring
4. Reinventing
5. Reevaluating
6. Refocusing
7. Regaining control

Reengineering

Reengineering is perhaps the most powerful technique for simplifying your life and increasing your productivity. In its simplest terms, it refers to process analysis: you make a list of every single step of any work process from beginning to end. Leave nothing out: include every step, no matter how small, that you take to get from the beginning to the end of any task. Then review this list carefully one step at a time. With every step, ask why are you doing this at all?

You will find that fully 30 percent of the steps of any activity can be eliminated in the first run-through. They do not pass the *why* test. They have been slipped in over time for no apparent reason. They probably seemed to be a good idea at the time, but they merely make the process more complicated, more time-consuming, and more expensive.

A major national insurance company found that it was taking thirty to sixty days to approve an application for an insurance policy from the field. During this time, many of the potential customers changed their minds or bought their policies from someone else. It was causing a lot of stress in the field and at the home office. As a result, the company decided to reengineer the process. They made a list of every step that an insurance application went through from the time it reached the head office to the time it was approved and the answer was relayed back to the agent. There were twenty steps. They found that the entire time spent on an individual policy was approximately seventeen minutes, but the twenty-five steps were taking anywhere from four to eight weeks.

The company simplified the process by dividing the steps among two people instead of twenty-four. One person did twenty-three of the steps, and the second person simply checked those steps to make sure there were no mistakes. Before the year was out, the company was able to turn around an insurance policy and give an answer within twenty-four hours of receipt. It was also able to eliminate twenty-two different jobs in the process.

Some years ago, Motorola reengineered the process by which they produced custom-made pagers for corporate customers. The process used to consume twelve to fourteen months from the time the order was placed until the time the pager was produced. Once the company reengineered the process, a customer could place an order with a Motorola representative, which was typed into a laptop computer, which sent the order directly to the factory. Within forty-five minutes after the order was placed, the first customized pager came off the production line and was on its way out that day by the first available mail. This one act of process reengineering helped to make Motorola the world leader in pagers and cellular telephones at the time.

What parts of your work can be simplified, downsized, outsourced, or eliminated? One of the most powerful simplification techniques is called *job compression by responsibility expansion*: compressing a whole series of jobs into a single job and making one person responsible for far more of the steps than before. Instead of having people checking people who are checking people who are checking people, you place all the responsibility on a single individual for the entire process.

You can use reengineering for yourself as well. Instead of shopping several times a week, picking up several different things as you need them, discipline yourself to organize your shopping so that you do it all at once with one trip, with each stop coordinated with each other stop. This alone can save you several hours each week.

In sales, you can completely reengineer your activities so that you are spending more and more time face-to-face with potential customers. You go through and eliminate or reduce every activity that is not contributing directly to customer contacts and sales.

Reorganization

The second R is *reorganization*, which you need to be doing continually in times of rapid change. It used to be that companies reorganized every couple of years. Today both companies and individuals have to be reorganizing as an ongoing process.

Reorganizing in its simplest terms requires continually looking for ways to get a higher level of output per unit of input. You constantly look for ways to increase productivity, performance, and results by shifting people and resources around so that they work together more efficiently and produce more at lower cost.

Restructuring

The third R, *restructuring*, requires continually moving resources away from lower-value activities toward higher-value activities. You keep thinking in terms of the most valuable things that you do in terms of your customers or results, and you continually shift resources away from the 80 percent of activities that contribute 20 percent of your results toward the 20 percent of activities that contribute 80 percent of your results.

Reinventing

The fourth R, *reinventing*, requires that you continually think about starting over again and beginning your career or building your department or business as if it were brand-new. Use the walk across the street method: Imagine that you were to walk across the street and start your business or career over again today, knowing what you now know. If you had no previous baggage or commitments holding you back, what would you do more of or less of? What would you start up again, and what would you discontinue? How could you reinvent yourself on a regular basis?

Reevaluating

The fifth R, *reevaluating*, requires that you continually examine your priorities and the results of your past decisions to see if they're still valid in light of your current responsibilities. Aristotle once said that all of wisdom is a combination of experience plus reflection. Reevaluating requires reflecting on your experiences and your knowledge before taking the next step. Otherwise you'll find yourself repeating what you have done in the past, whether it is effective or not.

Refocusing

The sixth R, *refocusing*, means bringing your resources to bear on the one or two things you can do that can make the greatest contribution to your life and your work. Your ability to focus and concentrate on your highest-value activities is the key to personal power and personal effectiveness.

Regaining Control

The final R is *regaining control.* You think through and simplify everything that you're doing based on what I've discussed in this chapter. As a result, you will experience a tremendous sense of power over your goals, your objectives, your activities, your staff, your resources, and your time.

Whenever you experience stress from having too much to do and too little time, it means that your life and your work are out of control in some way. Rather than accepting this as a fact of life, your job is to simplify your life in every way possible. Examine your areas of highest stress. What can you do in each of those areas to reduce the burden?

Simplifying your life is a never-ending process. Every day, every week, you should be looking for ways to reduce the amount of time and complexity necessary to achieve the results that are important to you. The better you get at simplification, the more you will get done, the happier you'll be, and the more you'll be paid.

Key Points

- The principle of simplicity: prepare clear, uncomplicated plans and clear, concise orders.
- Concentrate your time and energy on the things that make the most contribution to your life.
- Avoid being distracted into areas that contribute very little.
- Look for ways to reduce the time it takes to accomplish a task.
- Use lists to organize your goals and priorities.
- Take your most important task, and work on it till you are finished. Then proceed to the next task.
- Use a time planner.
- Fun, easy tasks usually contribute very little, but big, difficult tasks can have enormous consequences.
- Use the ABCDE method to rank your priorities.
- Eliminate tasks of low value.
- To simplify your life, get rid of things. When in doubt, throw it out.
- Work at a clear, clean workspace.

4

The Power of Concentration

Your ability to concentrate on one thing—the most important thing—and stay with it until it's complete is the single most important skill or discipline of success.

Self-discipline has been defined as the ability to make yourself do what you should do, when you should do it, whether you feel like it or not. Anybody can do something if and when they feel like doing it, but the person who can force himself to do it when he doesn't feel like it who will eventually win out.

Napoleon Hill, author of *Think and Grow Rich*, called self-discipline the master key to riches. It is a defining characteristic of all high-achieving men and women. Nowhere is self-discipline more important than in your ability to concentrate persistently and single-mindedly on your most important task until it's finished.

All great success comes about as the result of sustained concentration. Throughout the ages, the principle of mass—the concentration of combat power at the decisive place and time—has been the key to victory in warfare. Your personal ability to mass your forces and concentrate all of your energies on the one or two things that contribute most of your success is essential to everything you are and become. Napoleon once said that when you have resolved to fight the battle, collect your whole force; dispense with nothing; a single battalion sometimes decides the day.

Your ability to concentrate all of your best resources at the point of greatest opportunity—often your competitors' point of greatest vulnerability—can enable a smaller company to overwhelm a larger company. Apple Computer was able to create one of the most successful computer businesses in the world against the likes of IBM by focusing on its operating system.

Apple made it so easy to use its computers that millions of computer users were lured away from the IBM MS-DOS operating system, making Apple a multibillion-dollar business. IBM in turn concentrated on mainframes throughout the sixties and seventies, and by doing an outstanding job, dominated the entire world of mainframe computer sales.

Management guru Peter Drucker once wrote that whenever you see something getting done, you find a monomaniac with a mission. Every product, every service, every market, every company that is successful has a champion who is totally, fanatically committed to the success of that endeavor. Single-minded concentration may not guarantee success, but lack of single-minded concentration will virtually guarantee failure and underachievement.

One of the most important principles of the mass is deciding where to concentrate your forces. You cannot do everything at once. You cannot be everywhere at once. Your mental, physical, emotional, and financial resources are limited. You are always forced to choose the one or two things on which you are going to concentrate your energies, and your choice of those key areas is essential to your success.

To be successful in your work, you must achieve a minimum level of competence in your critical success factors: the things that you absolutely, positively have to do well in order to be successful. They are called *critical* because of failure in any one of them can be fatal to your career or business. Fortunately, there are only about five to seven critical success factors in any job, company, or area of activity.

In order to win in business and personal life, you have to identify your critical success factors. Then give yourself a grade in each factor and work on bringing up your score in the factors that may be holding you back.

Seven Critical Success Factors in Management

1. Planning
2. Organizing
3. Staffing
4. Delegating
5. Supervising
6. Measuring
7. Reporting

Seven Factors in Management Success

There are seven critical success factors in management: planning, organizing, staffing, delegating, supervising, measuring, and reporting. In planning, you decide exactly what your goals and objectives are and what resources you will need to attain them. In organizing, you decide exactly how you are going to acquire and deploy the resources you need to achieve the goals and objectives that have been assigned to you. In staffing, you select the key people that you will need to carry out the key responsibilities that must be fulfilled in achieving your goal. In delegating, you assign the right job to the right person in the right way at the right time. In supervising, you ensure that the jobs you have assigned are being done to the proper level of quality and on the correct schedule. In measuring, you continually monitor and evaluate results and compare them against projections and budgets. In reporting, you make sure that the critical parties in your work life are fully informed about your activities and their results.

A weakness in any one of these areas will act as a brake on your results and your career: it will stop you or hold you back. For example, you could be excellent at six of these seven critical success factors but be terrible at staffing: you may not be able to hire or keep the necessary people to get the job done. Your inability to recruit and staff appropriately can be fatal to your career: this is why it is called a critical success factor.

If you're in management, give yourself a score of one to ten on each of these critical success factors, with one being the lowest and ten being the highest. Then identify your weakest area and make a plan to bring it up.

The winning edge theory was one of the most important business concepts of the twentieth century. It says that small differences in ability can translate into enormous differences in results. Moreover, small improvements in a critical success factor area can lead to extraordinary differences in results, sometimes very quickly.

For example, many managers are poor at delegation. However, if you cannot delegate well, you cannot be effective as a manager. Taking a course, reading a book, listening to an audio program, or somehow bringing up your delegation skills can enable you to increase your ability and multiply your impact.

One of the most important principles in concentration is *leverage*. Your ability to leverage yourself multiplied by the people and resources under your control or influence, is the key to your business success. Successful leaders always think in terms of how their activities influence the activities, outcomes, and results of other people and situations. They're constantly engaging in what Warren Bennis, in his book *Leaders*, calls "self-deployment." Top people are experts at deploying themselves as valuable and scarce resources so that they can make the greatest possible contribution.

> **Seven Success Factors for Sales**
> 1. Prospecting
> 2. Establishing rapport and trust
> 3. Identifying the problem or need of the customer
> 4. Presenting your product or service as the ideal solution to the problem or need
> 5. Answering questions or concerns satisfactorily
> 6. Getting a commitment to take action
> 7. Getting referrals and repeat business

Success Factors in Sales

If you're in sales, you have seven critical success factors as well: prospecting; establishing rapport and trust; identifying the problem or need of the customer; presenting your product or service as the ideal solution to the problem or need; answering questions or concerns satisfactorily; getting a commitment to take action; and finally getting referrals and repeat business.

Your ability to excel in each of these areas is essential to your success as a salesperson. A weakness in any one of these areas can hold you back from using all your other skills and abilities.

For example, you could be very good at everything except prospecting. If you are poor at prospecting, it'll hold you back from using all of your other skills. Your entire career could be in jeopardy. Several people in my seminars have taken this idea to heart. They realized that they were poor in prospecting and that it was sabotaging their careers, so they decided to go to work to become excellent prospectors, and they did. One after another, they became some of the most successful and highest-paid people in their industries by resolutely attacking the area of prospecting until they were so good at it that they had far more people to see than they had hours available during the workday. If prospecting is a concern of yours, decide today to become so good at it that you have appointments all day, every day, with good prospects who can and will buy your product or service.

Some people are afraid of prospecting. The fear of rejection in selling is the primary reason salespeople fail, but the fear of rejection is a learned fear, and you can unlearn it by acting as if you had no fear at all. Go out and call on people, day after day, without being concerned whether or not they buy. In no time at all, you'll find yourself quite calm and relaxed about prospecting, and the sales will start to roll in.

Success Factors in Business

Here are some critical success factors if you run your own business: production, quality control, marketing, sales, finance, leadership, innovation, and distribution. It's up to you to identify the critical

> **Success Factors in Business**
>
> 1. Production
> 2. Quality control
> 3. Marketing
> 4. Sales
> 5. Finance
> 6. Leadership
> 7. Innovation
> 8. Distribution

things that your company does to ensure that it succeeds in a competitive market, and then identify where you are strong and where you are weak in each area.

However you are doing what you are doing today, you must be doing it considerably better one year from now. The absence of a commitment to continual improvement becomes an acceptance of mediocrity by default.

What is your limiting factor? What one skill or ability is determining the speed at which you achieve your goals? What is holding you back? What one talent or ability, if you developed it and did it in an excellent fashion, would have the greatest positive impact on your career?

This is a terribly important question. If you do not know what this one skill is—the one skill that can help you more than anything else—you must find out. You must honestly evaluate yourself and your own performance, or you must ask the people around you, but you must determine what it is and then set it as a goal, make a plan, and go to work to bring that skill up to a high level. If you become absolutely outstanding in an area that doesn't make any difference while remaining poor in an area that is critical to your success, it can trip you up and hold you back every step of the way.

The Battle of Gaugamela

Perhaps the greatest single example of the principle of the mass of concentration of forces took place at the Battle of Gaugamela on September 30, 331 BC, between the armies of Alexander the Great of Macedon and Darius III of Persia. Having lost two battles to Alexander (including, as we've seen, the Battle of Issus), Darius was determined not to lose the third battle, which he knew would be decisive for the Persian Empire. He therefore assembled an army of almost a million men north of Babylon and cleared the ground in front of his army so that his battle chariots would have a flat terrain on which to maneuver.

Alexander's army consisted of about 50,000 men and cavalry (although estimates vary). The odds against him were as much as twenty to one. His men were in high spirits, but they were obviously a bit uneasy at seeing the hundreds of thousands of Persian infantry and cavalry arrayed against them.

The night before the battle, Alexander gathered his chief officers to explain their roles in the coming conflict. Alexander believed in telling everyone exactly what was going to happen and exactly what they were expected to do when it happened. He assured his officers that they were going to win the next day. His officers wondered why he was so convinced of victory when faced with such a huge mass of well-armed Persian troops. Alexander explained that the army of Darius was made up of levies of troops from all over the Persian Empire. None of them had any loyalty to each other. They were only loyal to Darius.

Alexander was convinced that if Darius were to be removed, the Persian army would fall apart, so he told his generals to pass the word down the line that the next day they would not try to defeat the entire Persian army. There was only one order of battle, one command: the next day, the entire Macedonian army was to go out, follow Alexander, and kill Darius. The message was passed down the line from soldier to soldier. They would not have to worry about defeating the entire Persian army. They would just wait until the critical moment and then follow Alexander in a thrust into the Persian center, where Darius was commanding the Persian forces. Their job was simple. It was to kill Darius.

The next morning as the sun rose, Darius and the Persians saw that the Macedonian army was lined up at an oblique angle to the Persian front. As the Macedonians began to move to their right toward the left flank of the Persians, the Persian battle chariots were ordered to the attack, but Alexander was ready with professional javelin throwers and archers who showered missiles down on the chariots and horses, destroying most of them. As Alexander had expected, this left an opening in the Persian center. Alexander then turned to his companion guard of 6,000 crack Macedonian cavalry and shouted, "Now follow me, and let us kill Darius!" Like a spear, with Alexander as the point, the Macedonian cavalry plunged into the center of the Persian army. The Persians with their large, unwieldy forces were unable to bring reserves in to protect the front, where Darius was most vulnerable.

As Alexander and his Macedonians broke through the front lines and approached the encampment of Darius, Darius jumped on a horse and fled from the scene of the battle. Not wanting to be left alone, his top generals jumped on their horses and chariots as well and followed after him. When the word went out that Darius and his generals were fleeing the scene of battle and the Macedonians had already broken the front lines, the Persian army began to disintegrate, as expected. By the end of the day, the Persian army had been destroyed and scattered in all directions. The Persian Empire collapsed, and Alexander became the master of perhaps the greatest and richest empire in history. He was twenty-three years old.

Alexander knew that his outnumbered army could not defeat the mass of Persians, especially since he was hundreds of miles from his home in Macedonia and his supply base on the Mediterranean. He committed his entire army to the one point of intensity where victory would make all the difference. By attacking Darius with such vigor that he fled, Alexander made the Persian army come apart, and the Macedonians, though greatly outnumbered, achieved one of the greatest victories in military history.

The Macedonian victory decided whether it would be Greek or Persian culture that would have such a great impact on Europe and Western civilization. The Battle of Gaugamela was a turning point that still affects us today.

The battles you fight each day are not as intense or as consequential as the great battles that decided the fate of nations and empires, but the same qualities that ensured victory to them apply to your activities as well. Your goals are to enjoy superb levels of physical health and have great relationships with the important people in your life. You want to do work that makes a difference and to do it well. Finally, you want to achieve a high level of financial independence so that you are not beholden to anyone.

The chief distinguishing characteristic of leaders throughout the ages is intensity of purpose. If you take two people of the same talents and abilities and give them the same opportunities, the person who wants it the most and the longest and the hardest will eventually win out. One key to success is desire—intense burning desire for a goal. The more intensely you want it, the more likely you are to discipline yourself to do whatever it takes to achieve it.

You can do specific things to attaining your goals, whatever they happen to be, that are far more valuable and important than other things. You cannot do everything, but you can do one thing—the most important thing—and you can stay with it until it's complete.

The purpose of strategic thinking and strategic planning in business is financial: to increase the return on equity, or ROE. It is also to improve the relative correlation of forces between yourself and your competitors. The proper result of strategy is that you are better off financially after implementing it than you were before.

In your personal life, your goal is to increase your return on energy. Your capital is mental, emotional, and physical. Your job is to get the highest possible return on the investment of yourself and your energies.

You could say that all of life is a trade: you are continually trading your time for the rewards that you enjoy. At any given time, you can look around you and total up your tangible and intangible assets to determine how well you have traded your time up until now. For example, if you are thirty years old, you have been working for ten years, and your net worth is $20,000, you have traded each of those working years for $2,000, plus expenses. Is this a good trade or not? If someone offered you $2,000 per year plus expenses to work for them, would you take it? If you have only accumulated $2,000 per year for the last ten years, that is the trade that you've been making.

However, one of the most important rules of success is this: it doesn't matter where you're coming from; all that really matters is where you're going. If you're not happy with how well you have traded in the past, it's up to you to trade better in the future. If you're not happy with your current return on energy, it's up to you to improve the quality and quantity of your services and concentrate your energy single-mindedly where you can get a higher return in the months and years ahead. Concentrating your powers—your ability to think, decide, and to discipline yourself to deploy your energies for a higher and better return—is central to your success and happiness.

Fortunately, when you are concentrating single-mindedly on high-value activities, you feel much better and happier about yourself. Concentrated work on high value-activities actually releases energy and makes you feel stronger and more powerful. Once you get into it, you feel better and better about yourself. Eventually, you will condition yourself—train yourself in such a way that you will be impatient with low-value activities. You will find it easy to discipline yourself to do more and more of the things that have higher and higher payoffs.

I was talking to a gentleman who told me this was exactly what he had experienced over the last few years. When he started working on his personal and professional development, he was making $21,000 per year. Last year, he told me that he had made just over $540,000. He also said that now he finds that he has little or no interest in television, radio, newspapers, or idle conversation. His reference group, the people with whom he associates, has changed as well. He has become impatient with attention relieving activities because he values himself much more highly than he did before. The more he accomplishes, the more he wants to accomplish. The more he achieves, the more he likes and respects himself, and therefore the higher goals and standards he sets for himself. Like cream, he is rising to the top and becoming an outstanding person.

The same thing will happen to you almost naturally as you begin to think of yourself as a leader, set clear goals and objectives, become action oriented, take the offensive to achieve your goals, and continually concentrate on those few things that can make the greatest contribution to your life.

Here's a good question for you: Why are you on the payroll? What have you been hired to accomplish? Most people given a piece of paper and asked that question will jot down all of the activities they engage in during the day. However, activities are merely inputs. You have been hired to achieve outputs, sometimes called your key result areas. These are the things that you absolutely, positively have to accomplish in order to stay on the payroll. They are measurable, time bounded, and completely under your control. You are responsible for them. When you apply the 80/20 rule to your work, you'll find that 20 percent of your outputs account for 80 percent of the contribution that you make. And here's a real problem for most people: even if you become outstanding at doing the 80 percent of things that only contribute 20 percent of your results, you'll still fail in your career.

Many people make the mistake of investing effort in becoming better and better at things that are less and less important to achieving their real goals, but this is not for you. In concentrating your energies, you focus on the one or two things where excellent performance can bring extraordinary results. You focus on becoming better and better at the one or two things that can have the greatest positive impact on your life and career.

What are your highest-value activities, both at work and in your personal life? What do you do that gives you the highest return on energy? What do you do that enables you to be a multiplication sign and leverage yourself in your activities?

You do many things all day long, and you're extremely good at some of them; moreover the consequences of your success in those areas affects many other people as well. What are they? What can you and only you do that will make a real difference if done well? What are the things that you and only you can do? If you don't do them, no one else will, and if they're done really well, they will make a real difference in your life.

There's only one answer to this question at any given time. Your ability to identify that one thing and throw your whole heart into doing it well will make all the difference to your future. The British economist John Maynard Keynes once wrote that you should give a lot of thought to the future, because you'll be spending the rest of your life there.

In concentrating your forces, you have to give a lot of thought to your future as well. Leaders think about the future; indeed only leaders can do that. Everyone else depends upon what and how well the leader thinks about the future and about where the organization is going. If you want to be a leader, you have to think the way a leader thinks. Where do you want to be in three to five years? What critical success factors or abilities will you need to develop to ensure that you get there? What customers are you serving today, and what customers will you be serving tomorrow? What will your customers of tomorrow need, want, or expect from you? What will your competitors be offering to your customers to get their business? What additional skills, abilities, or core competencies will you or your organization have to develop to achieve victory in the marketplace of tomorrow?

Keys to Industry Dominance

In their book *The Disciplines of Market Leaders*, Michael Treacy and Fred Wiersema conclude that successful companies are excellent in one of three areas; expertise or dominance in one of these can lead to dominance of the entire industry, especially in terms of customer retention and profitability. The first of these three areas is customer intimacy: the company's ability to establish high-quality relationships with its customers, characterized by an in-depth knowledge of the customer's situation and needs. As a salesperson, this is where you can achieve a core competency that can enable you to win against competition of all kinds. A second area of strategic excellence is a reputation for product innovation and quality. Companies like Sony can charge more for their products because of their reputation for innovation and excellence. The third discipline of market leaders is operational excellence. This could refer to a McDonald's or a Walmart, whose ability to do business at the lowest possible cost enables them to be a low-price leader in a mass market.

In each case, market dominance arises from an ability to concentrate single-mindedly on achieving superiority in a particular area. The authors also observe that it is impossible to excel in more than one key area. In order to dominate their marketplace, each individual or company has to maintain a high level of quality in two areas while achieving excellence in the third.

What does this mean to you? If you are in sales, entrepreneurship, or a small- or medium-sized business, your major advantage is your ability to get close to your customer, to establish customer intimacy. At the same time, you must conduct your business economically and efficiently, with good time and cost management. You must offer good quality products and services to stand behind, but your area of concentration is probably customer intimacy.

If you own your own company, you have to ask what type, range, variety, and quality of products and services you will need to be offering to your customers three to five years from now.

You need to be asking what size you want to grow to and what kind of financial results you want from your operations.

As an individual, one of your goals should be financial independence. So a good question is, what is my plan to get my finances under control and build a financial fortress during the course of my working lifetime?

When are you going to start on your plan? The number one reason for financial failure in America is procrastination. Everyone wants to be financially independent, but they lack the discipline to concentrate single-mindedly on putting away a certain amount of their income on a regular basis.

The most important attitude for guaranteeing financial success is long-term perspective. Your ability to take the long term into consideration engaging in your day-to-day activities is the key to your long-term success. The best formula for success is long-term vision combined with short-term focus.

When you have established long-term objectives, such as financial independence, business and career success, good health and happiness for your family, you can make plans to attain those goals. Then every day, make sure that what you are doing every minute is the highest and best use of your time and energy in moving you toward those long-term goals.

Perhaps the most important question in time management is, what is the most valuable use of my time right now? Make sure that every hour of every day you are working on the answer to that question. Never give in to the temptation to clear up small things first. What is the most valuable use of my time right now?

The Reverse Salient

In military theory, there is a principle called the *reverse salient*. Normally, a salient is where one force makes a breakthrough into the lines of the opposing force. The salient is like a bulge or protrusion where a breakthrough is possible if it can be reinforced and exploited. A reverse salient has the opposite effect: the entire line has moved forward except for one area, where the enemy is holding out. This reverse salient can be a great danger because it can hold back your entire line. If it is properly reinforced by the enemy, the enemy can break out in your rear and surround you.

In business, we have reverse salients as well. These are the areas that are holding us back from realizing our full potential. Sometimes your reverse salient can be a specific skill or ability. It can involve a specific relationship or person. It can be associated with a specific competitor or competitive product or service. It is the one thing that, if it were resolved satisfactorily, would enable you to move ahead far more rapidly than you are today.

Do you have a reverse salient? What is it? Sometimes your ability to identify it and concentrate single-mindedly on eliminating it can give you the winning edge. Sometimes your ability to eliminate the one thing that is holding you back can help you more than anything else.

All extraordinary accomplishment is preceded by thousands of ordinary accomplishments that nobody ever sees or appreciates. Your ability to concentrate your forces on the goals, activities, skills, and areas of high value that can contribute the most to your life is the key to achieving great success. Once you've decided upon your point of intensity, your critical success factor, your key result area, or the one thing that you and only you can do that, if done well, will make a real difference, throw your whole heart into it, and stay with it until it's 100 percent complete. When you can discipline yourself to do that, you will become unstoppable.

Key Points

- Concentrate on the most important thing and stay with it until it's complete.
- Self-discipline is the ability to make yourself do what you should do, when you should do it, whether you feel like it or not.
- Self-discipline is the master key to riches.
- Concentrate your forces at the single most important point.
- Identify your critical success factors.
- Weakness in any key area will act as a brake on your results.
- Small improvements in a critical area can lead to extraordinary differences in results.
- Top people are experts at deploying themselves as valuable and scarce resources.

5

Unity of Command

One of the most important principles in military strategy—and the key to the success or failure of any business or enterprise—is the principle of unity of command. This means that for every objective, there should be unity of effort under one responsible commander. A single individual should be responsible for the activities of the group. Every person should report to only one person. It should be absolutely clear who your boss is and what your boss expects of you. Every person who reports to you should be absolutely clear about what they're expected to do and by when and to what standard.

During the Iranian hostage situation in 1979, an entire U.S. embassy full of personnel was seized and held by the Iranians for many months. Finally, the U.S. military decided to launch a rescue attempt in Iran. This rescue attempt was an unmitigated disaster. Its failure was the result of all of the parties violating the principles of strategy and warfare, especially and including the failure to unify the entire operation under a single commander. Because of political considerations, the coming election, and just plain incompetence, all the armed forces were involved in this military operation.

This included elements of the Army, Navy, Air Force, Marines, and even the Coast Guard. Each of these military units had their own commanders, who were often working at cross purposes with the other commanders, with everyone determined to get their share of the glory. Each of the forces used their own equipment, much of which was incompatible with other equipment. They failed to have sufficient spare parts available in case of breakdowns. Insufficient advance intelligent work was done so that the different forces landed in different places and were unable to coordinate their activities. On top of all of this, the entire operation was being second-guessed by President Jimmy Carter and his generals from the Pentagon by satellite. No one knew what was going on or who was in charge at any given time. The objectives were unclear, confused, or contradictory. No one had the final authority to solve any problems or to take any action. Offensive operations never got underway, and there was never any ability to mass and concentrate the U.S. forces to implement the rescue attempt.

Eleven years later, the exact opposite situation took place. The Iraqi army invaded and seized the Kuwaiti oil fields. When they refused to withdraw, President George H.W. Bush, in conjunction with chief of staff Colin Powell, appointed General Norman Schwarzkopf to be in complete charge of getting the Iraqi army out of Kuwait. From the first minute that General Schwarzkopf arrived in the Persian Gulf to take command, there was no question about who was in charge. From the beginning to the end of both the Desert Shield and Desert Storm operations, General Schwarzkopf was in command of the entire operation. After proper preparation, the military attack and offensive came off smoothly, efficiently, and fast. The second largest army in the world knocked out forty-one of forty-two divisions of the world's fourth largest army in less than 100 hours. One of the most important reasons for this success was the unity of command practiced throughout the entire Gulf War.

When Chrysler Corporation got into severe financial difficulties in the early 1980s, the company had thirty-six vice presidents, each of which ran their independent areas like private kingdoms, with no one reporting to anyone else. The president of the company at that time spent most of his time playing personalities and politics amongst the various power centers throughout the world organization. As a result, the company came right to the brink of collapse.

In desperation, the board of directors fired the president and asked Lee Iacocca, past president of Ford Corporation, to step in and take charge. When Iacocca arrived on the scene, Chrysler Corporation had monthly cash requirements of $250 million, and it only had $1 million in the bank. It owed money to 450 banks and had 641,000 people on the payroll throughout the world. The company had more than 4,000 dealerships and hundreds of small and large companies whose survival depended on supplying Chrysler with the parts required to manufacture its cars and trucks.

The situation was desperate, and most financial analysts predicted that Chrysler would collapse. At that time, Chrysler creditors were expecting to get back maybe 10 cents on the dollar.

When Lee Iacocca arrived on the scene, he immediately took charge like a commanding general. His objective was clear: to save Chrysler. He went on the offensive the first day. He immediately began negotiating for breathing room with the banks. He negotiated givebacks and concessions from the hundreds of thousands of union members. He went to Washington and got backing from both the Congress and the Senate for a $1.2 billion loan guarantee, to be repaid over five years. He went on television and asked people to purchase Chrysler cars. He traveled throughout the Chrysler organization and asked the workers to cooperate with him to save the company.

The result? From a company on the verge of collapse, Chrysler did a complete turnaround. The company paid back all of its loans in twenty-two months, not five years, including $350 million in interest to the banks, who had only been expecting to get 10 back cents on each dollar. Almost 650,000 jobs were saved, and Chrysler Corporation regained its position as one of the strongest manufacturing companies in the world. The critical factor was the unity of command under Lee Iacocca at the critical moment of decision.

The late business executive Al Dunlap, whose nickname was "Chainsaw Al," developed a remarkable ability to turn around companies that were on the verge of collapse. When nothing else could be done and the company appeared to be facing either slow decline or bankruptcy, Al Dunlap was called in and put in command.

Dunlap explained that his method of turnaround was quite simple. From the day he arrived on the scene, he took complete charge of all operations. All nonperforming divisions or departments of the company were cut back or shut down. All nonperforming executives or staff were let go. He then focused all of the company's energy and resources on its most profitable areas of activity. He brought in top people and put them in command in key divisions of the organization. In a year or two, he turned billion-dollar losses into billion-dollar profits, increased the share value of the stock three, four, or five times, and transformed the company into a top competitor in a tough market.

Top teams in every sport are the same: they have clear coaching and leadership. Everyone knows who calls the plays. Everyone knows who's in charge. Everyone knows who the leader is.

Everyone wants and needs to be under the authority of someone else. It is essential for the efficient function of any organization that everyone knows the chain of command, whom they report to, and what is expected of them.

To break through your success barriers, you must aspire to a leadership role. You must develop the ability to persuade and influence others to work with you to achieve your goals. Becoming a leader requires understanding the roles and responsibilities of leadership and practicing the qualities of leadership until you begin to emerge as a leader in your personal and business life.

For many years, the "great man theory of history" prevailed. This theory is summarized by saying that all of history is the biographies of great men and women. This means that the course of human history has largely been determined by the actions and decisions of specific individuals at critical times throughout the years.

Sometimes one decision by one leader at a specific moment in time has led to the rise or the fall of an entire empire. On June 28, 1914, the Archduke Franz Ferdinand of Austria-Hungary was assassinated in Sarajevo, in present-day Bosnia. Austria-Hungary used this as an excuse for declaring war on neighboring Serbia and its ally, Russia. World War I had begun. Four years later, the Austro-Hungarian Empire, which had lasted for almost 800 years, collapsed. The Ottoman Empire of Turkey, along with the Russian Empire, collapsed as well. A single decision taken in response to a single act of violence ushered in thirty years of warfare that changed Europe and the world forever.

You regularly make critical decisions that have enormous consequences for your life. The choice of course of study in school can determine the direction of your life for many years. So can the choice of a job or a spouse.

You are always free to choose. The ability to take command and assume a leadership role in your own life entails tremendous responsibilities. In fact, your entire life is the sum total result of the choices and decisions that you have made up to this moment. Leaders are simply those who make better choices and better decisions more often than not.

Sometimes I ask my audiences, how many people here are in sales? In an average audience, perhaps 20–25 percent of the participants will raise their hands. I then point out that everyone is in sales: everyone is in the business of communicating, persuading, influencing, and negotiating with others. The only question is whether or not you are any good at it. Everyone is a leader and a decision-maker at some level. The only question is whether or not you are any good at it.

The good news is that leaders are usually made, not born. They are largely self-made as a result of continually working on themselves over the years. No one starts off as a leader, but you can aspire to leadership by learning what leaders do and how they think and feel and by copying them until you become one yourself.

Three Forms of Power

1. Position power
2. Expert power
3. Ascribed power

Three Forms of Power

There are three major forms of power used by leaders today. The first is called *position power*. This refers to the powers of rewarding and punishing that go along with a particular title or role. If you are a sales manager or vice president of marketing, you have the power to hire and fire people, to raise their pay or leave it where it is. You have the power to hand out privileges or punishments and to alter the terms and conditions of employment to make them more agreeable or less agreeable. These powers do not belong to you personally, but to whoever has your title. They are conferred by the title itself. They go with the position.

The second type of power is *expert power*. Expert power arises when you are very good at what you do; as a result people defer to your opinion and your judgment. Experts in critical areas for the survival or growth of organizations have tremendous power. Even though they may have no staff at all, their decisions and judgments carry a tremendous weight.

One of the most important decisions you make during the course of your working life is to develop expert power in what you do. By becoming supremely good in your area of expertise, you develop power out of all proportion to your position or title. The most respected and valued people in any organization are those who have developed the ability to make the most valuable and most consistent contributions to the business. By becoming excellent at what you do, you set up a force field of energy or magnetism that attracts power and respect to you.

The third form of power is called *ascribed power*: power that is conferred upon you by others because they like you, trust you, believe in you, and want you to have more influence and authority. Ascribed power is a combination of being very good at what you do, being likable, being results-oriented, and being perceived as the kind of person who can be the most useful to others in helping them to achieve their individual goals.

It's been said that leadership is the ability to amass followers. After World War II, virtually all of the heads of major companies were ex–military officers. They had been taught a command and control structure of leadership from the top down. The levels of leadership were organized in a hierarchy from the top person down to the bottom people. Each person was expected to do as he or she was told. Organizations were run very much like armies, with managers and executives taking the place of the generals and officers.

Today all that has changed. People still need structure in which to work, but today they demand a much higher level of democracy and involvement in order to perform at their best. They will only perform for a person if they like them and feel that they are the best person to lead the organization. If not, the people below the leadership level have a hundred different ways to sabotage the leader's effectiveness and often to ensure their departure.

I worked for a company once that had brought in a president from the outside. He considered himself superior to people who had worked in the organization for many years. Instead of working by consensus through the experienced executives under him, he made his own decisions separate and apart from the opinions and insights of others. Instead of asking people to do things, he told them. In no time at all, he had built up a huge reservoir of resentment throughout the organization that slowly but inevitably led to his being forced out of an extremely highly paid position.

The effective leader begins with the needs of the situation. The effective leader asks, what does this situation most require of me? What am I uniquely capable of contributing to this organization? Of all the things that I can bring, what are the one or two things that I and only I can do that will make a real difference?

Vision and Excellence

I have said that the most common characteristic of leadership throughout the ages is vision. Leaders can see the big picture. They can project forward three to five years and clearly imagine where they want to take the organization and what it will look like when they get there. Leaders have the ability to articulate this vision in such a way that everyone around them can see and understand where they're going.

The Bible says, "Where there is no vision, the people perish." This doesn't mean that they physically lie down and die, but that they lose their spirit and enthusiasm for the future. The leader is able to articulate an exciting vision of a compelling future that everyone wants to be a part of.

Perhaps the most compelling vision that you can articulate for the people around you is the determination to be the best at whatever you do. Long, complicated mission statements are usually not very effective in motivating people, because no one really understands them or relates them to their own personal situations. But a mission statement or vision of being the best in your business or industry offers something that people can get excited about. Everyone wants to be a part of a company or department that is committed to excellence.

In the presence of a vision that motivates and excites people, they will work harder and better and produce more and of higher quality than under any other set of circumstances. Without a vision, people fall into an operational mode of working, looking at the job as a nine-to-five activity and going home without giving it much further thought.

A vision or mission statement should be short, sweet, and to the point. For example, if you ask anyone at Coca-Cola Corporation worldwide what their mission is, they will say simply that it is to beat Pepsi. On the other hand, if you ask anyone in the PepsiCo organization what their corporate mission is, they will tell you that it is to beat Coke. The countless individuals in these organizations worldwide will engage in a thousand different activities, but they're all crystal clear that the aim of all their activities is to win—to be the best, to achieve victory over their biggest rival.

Leaders focus on the needs of the situation before thinking about their own needs or wants or desires. They also focus on the results required of the organization and how they themselves can best contribute to achieving those results.

What results are expected of you? What results are expected of your organization or your department? If you were completely successful in your activities, what would happen? What would success look like? How would you describe complete success in your work or your company?

Leaders focus on strengths, in both themselves and others. Strong people have far more weaknesses than strengths. You can never achieve greatness by simply compensating for your weaknesses, but you can become outstanding by identifying your areas of greatest potential strength and then focusing all of your energies on becoming outstanding in those few areas.

You succeed at what you do because you excel in a few core competencies. These are key skill areas where as a result of natural ability, education, experience, and training, you have become very proficient. These core competencies are like the axles around which your career turns. They are the central skills that make it possible for you to do your job in the first place.

Unity of Command

Every organization ideally begins with a series of core competencies that enable it to bring products and services to the market of such a quality and quantity that it outsells and outdelivers the competition.

Your core competencies as an individual or organization are the foundation upon which you build future success, but your core competencies are rapidly becoming obsolete. Some of the best work in strategy today focuses on identifying the core competencies that you'll require three to five years from now in order to win the competitive battles in the marketplace that will be taking place at that time.

Look at the trends in your industry. Which direction is the market going in? What will your customers be wanting three to five years from today? What will you have to be very, very good at, both personally and as an organization, in order to win against determined opposition at that time?

During the 1930s, while Hitler was rearming and the possibility of another war was looming in Europe, the American administration under Franklin D. Roosevelt was promising never to send American soldiers to war again. But behind the scenes, General George C. Marshall, head of the Joint Chiefs of Staff, was aware that a war was coming and that America would have to be prepared to fight effectively in it. While the French were pouring their money into the Maginot Line, a system of fortifications from the Swiss border to the Belgian border, in order to forestall a German attack, the American military began to develop a tank corps under the command of a colonel from Arizona named George S. Patton Jr.

While the French were busy preparing to fight World War I, both the Germans and the Americans were aware that any subsequent war would be a war of movement, largely dictated by tank or armies that would break through or go around fixed defenses.

When the Germans swept into France in 1940, the French Republic collapsed within six weeks; all of its defenses turned out to be completely useless. For twenty years, France had poured all of its resources into developing core competencies that were now obsolete. The Germans, on the other hand, had learned the lessons of mobility and lightning warfare, supported and driven by mechanized units.

What core competencies will you need in the future? Remember, only the leader can think about the future; everyone else depends upon the accuracy with which the leader thinks about and plans for the future.

Leading by Example

One of the most important qualities of leadership is to lead by example, to be a role model, to be the kind of person that everyone else looks up to and wants to be like. Leaders they carry themselves at all times as leaders, even when no one is watching.

If you want the people under you to treat others well, you must treat others well even when you don't feel like it. If you want others to be punctual, you must be punctual. If you want others to use their time well, you must use your time well. If you want others to run efficient and effective meetings, you must run efficient and effective meetings whenever you are in charge. If you want others to treat each other with respect and politeness, you must practice respect and politeness in all of your interactions.

The leader lives in a goldfish bowl. Everyone is watching. Everyone is continually weighing, criticizing, and evaluating your behavior. Nothing is missed or goes unremarked. Your slightest comment or observation or behavior is immediately noticed and relayed to everyone.

Leaders are very aware of the impact of their words and gestures on the people around them. You must always be sensitive to the fact that everything you say or do is magnified times the people who report to you or who look up to you for guidance. A positive remark from you to someone over whom you exert influence or control has inordinately positive effects. A negative remark or criticism has inordinately negative effects. Choose your words and your behavior with care.

Integrity

Perhaps the most important and respected quality of leadership is integrity. It is the most admired quality of all people, especially of leaders. Trust binds all relationships together. The willingness and ability to trust the people that you look up to and report to is absolutely essential to your ability to perform at your very best.

Sometimes people tell me that they like their jobs, but they don't particularly like their bosses. I tell them that one of the most important things for success at work is to choose your boss with care. I've seen very few occasions where a person has been successful under a negative or dishonest boss. In most cases, you are wasting your life and career by staying in a situation with a negative or untrustworthy person, because it has no future.

Shakespeare wrote, "This above all, to thy own self be true, / And it must follow, as the night the day, / Thou canst then not be false to any man." More than anything else, you must be true to yourself in everything that you say and do. You must live in truth with yourself and others. You must be impeccably honest in all of your interactions and relationships. There's probably no area where people are more unforgiving than in regard to honesty and integrity, especially on the part of managers, parents, and leaders at every level. On the other hand, the most admired people in our society are those who are known for their absolute adherence to integrity under all circumstances.

Everything in life is a test. You are always being tested. Every single difficulty or problem that you experience is a test. Every problem person that you deal with is a test. Every great success or achievement is a test as well. The only question is whether or not you pass: how do you perform and behave when life goes for you or against you and everyone is watching?

One thing that is inevitable in the life of the leader is the crisis. Every small company has a crisis every two or three months that can sink the company if it is not responded to quickly and effectively. Crises are inevitable. The only question—and the only thing that really matters—is what you do when the inevitable crisis comes upon you. The best leaders regularly engage in crisis anticipation exercises with regard to every part of their lives and businesses.

Crisis anticipation requires that you look down the road of your life and ask yourself, what could possibly go wrong? Then, applying Murphy's Law, you ask, of all the things that could go wrong, what is the worst possible thing that could go wrong?

When I did this exercise with a corporation, they found that 40 percent of their sales were coming from one customer. When I asked them what was the worst thing that could go wrong, they replied immediately that it would be the loss of this customer. It could cripple or even break the business.

Then I asked them the second question: what steps can you take today to ensure that the worst possible outcome does not occur? They understood immediately. They began to focus more of their energies on aggressively developing other large customers until within two years, their major customer represented only 15 percent of their business. This decision and its results lowered the level of stress and tension within the organization and greatly increased the company's competitiveness in the marketplace.

Five Principles of Leadership

1. Clear objectives
2. Shared values and principles
3. Shared plans of action
4. Leading the action
5. Regular evaluation and measurement

Five Principles of Leadership

There are five steps that have been identified over the years in hundreds of situations that you can use to become an outstanding leader in your company or organization. These five principles have been developed as a result of millions of dollars of research invested in studying high-performing teams led by peak performing leaders.

The first key to maximum performance of your team is *clear objectives* defined, discussed, and agreed upon by everyone. Everyone has to know exactly why they're on the payroll and what they're expected to contribute to the overall results of the organization. The objectives must be specific, detailed, and measurable. They must be time bounded. They must have schedules with specific deadlines and with specific activities assigned to each person.

The second key to peak performing leadership is *shared values and principles*. Everyone must agree upon the values of the organization. Each of these values must be defined in terms of what it actually means in practice. Values are best discussed and agreed upon by each person. They are then organized and defined so that everyone knows what they are and can recognize whether they are adhered to or not.

The third step in peak performing leadership is *shared plans of action*. Each person must have specific roles and goals. Each person must have specific responsibilities for the completion of activities that contribute to the success of the overall goals and objectives of the team or company.

The fourth key to peak performance leadership is to *lead* the action. As a leader, your job is to go forward, set an example, be a role model. Your role as the leader is to take care of the people for whom you are responsible; it is to make sure that they have everything that they need to perform at their very best. Only you have the power and the authority to do this.

The final key to peak performance in leadership is *regular evaluation and measurement*. Ask constantly, how are we doing? Constantly evaluate and appraise your performance against your standards. When you run a business, your external measure of success is customer satisfaction and retention. Your internal measure of success is how happy and productive your people are. Your job is to work on both areas simultaneously, taking good care of the people who look up to you and of the customers upon whom your business depends.

Ralph Waldo Emerson once said that a great society is a society where men and women think greatly of their responsibilities. You become a leader in your life by thinking of yourself as a leader and then by practicing the leadership qualities of vision, courage, integrity, realism, and responsibility. You become a leader by thinking about the future and developing a clear plan for how you're going to get from where you are to where you want to go. You become a leader by treating your people so well that they want you to be in charge, that they want you to be the leader, because they see you as the person who can most help them achieve their goals.

Above all, when put into a leadership position, you take command. You refuse to make excuses or blame other people. You take charge; you refuse to criticize or complain. You take full control of the situation and accept responsibility for results. You walk, talk, think, and act like a leader, and as a result, you break through your success barriers.

> ### Key Points
> - Every objective requires unity of effort under one single commander.
> - It is essential for everyone to know the chain of command.
> - Your entire life is the sum total result of the choices you have made up to this moment.
> - Everyone is in the sales business.
> - There are three forms of power: position power, expert power, and ascribed power.
> - Leadership is the ability to amass followers.
> - Mission statements should be short, sweet, and to the point.
> - Leaders focus on strengths in both themselves and others.
> - Your core competencies are the foundation for your future success.
> - Integrity is the most admired quality, especially in leaders.
> - Avoid working for a negative or untrustworthy boss.
> - Everything in life is a test.
> - Five principles of leadership: clear objectives; shared values and principles; shared plans of action; leading the action; regular evaluation and measurement.

6

Gather Intelligence

One of the most important keys to breaking through your success barriers is included in the military principle of *intelligence*. This principle of war requires that you do everything possible to determine the dispositions, plans, strengths, and weaknesses of the enemy, as well as the terrain and all other factors which determine the outcome of the engagement. The gathering, analysis, and disposition of military intelligence can often determine the winning or losing of a great battle or even a war. In 2023, the United States allocated nearly $100 billion for its intelligence budget, an amount equal to the gross national product of some small countries.

In World War II, the British captured a machine, called Enigma, that was used to encode and decode German messages. The cracking of this code was exceptionally difficult, but it was accomplished. This became one of the top secrets of the war, and an entire department was set up outside of London to feed German radio traffic through this machine and decipher it. This enabled the Allies to accurately anticipate the German military plans in ways that were vital to the war effort.

The secrecy surrounding the Enigma Project was so great that when the British picked up the message that the German Air Force was going to bomb the city of Coventry, they allowed the bombing to go ahead without warning to the civilian population rather than take the chance that the Germans would discover that an Enigma machine had fallen into British hands.

Sometimes a single piece of information can have a major impact on the outcome of a battle or even a war. In the Pacific theater of World War II, the Japanese naval mastermind was Admiral Isoroku Yamamoto, who planned and led the attack on Pearl Harbor. As a result of an intercepted radio message, the allies learned that Yamamoto would be visiting a Japanese base in the Pacific, flying in on a specific schedule for the meeting. Armed with this piece of information, the American Air Force was able to dispatch a tightly planned mission that shot down the plane and killed Admiral Yamamoto. The loss of this one officer was a major blow to the Japanese war effort in the Pacific.

In business and in personal life, your ability to gather information about what is going on in your arena can be indispensable to your success or failure. American corporations spend more than $1 billion each year doing market research and analysis to determine exactly what products to develop, for what customers, with what features, and at what price they are most likely to be successful in the marketplace.

Today, in the information age, your ability to continually upgrade your information, knowledge, and skills is critical to your success. One piece of information at the right time can enable you to make a breakthrough that will give you a market lead that your competitors will not be able to match.

> **The I3 Model of Power**
>
> Information   Intelligence   Ideas

Management consultant Charles Handy talks about the I3 model of power and success in the information age. *I3* stands for *information, intelligence,* and *ideas.* The gathering of information from all sources, synthesized and distilled by experience, leads to higher levels of intelligence on the part of the person who has it. Higher levels of intelligence lead to a greater quality and quantity of ideas. And ideas are the true source of wealth for you today and in the future.

There's a direct relationship between the quantity of new ideas that you come up with and the quality of the ideas that will eventually result from them. Each person has about four ideas each year driving to and from work that, if acted upon, could make them a millionaire. In times of rapid growth of information and technology, more and more opportunities are opening up for people to make breakthroughs in their work and lives. Sometimes one insight is all you need to change your entire future.

Walt Disney, television personality Art Linkletter, and their wives were visiting Denmark in the early 1950s. One afternoon they visited the famous Tivoli Gardens, a family amusement and recreation park in Copenhagen. Walt Disney was fascinated by the fact that the entire Tivoli Gardens was so meticulously laid out and clean. It was teeming with families of parents and children having a good time. Every single light on every display worked perfectly.

Disney turned to Linkletter and said, "Someday, I'm going to build a park like this in America."

From then on, this idea became a burning obsession for Disney. The concept of Disneyland was born. Disneyland and later Disney World in Orlando, Florida, became the two most successful amusement parks in the world. They formed the foundation for the great Disney empire, which stretches around the globe. The entire Disneyland empire was largely triggered by that one observation and the idea that it sparked in the mind of Walt Disney.

In your work, it's absolutely vital to get the facts on an ongoing basis. It's also important to get the real facts and refuse to settle for the apparent facts, the assumed facts, the hoped for facts, the accepted facts, or even the previous facts. The late CEO of General Electric Jack Welch called this the *reality principle*. His question in every new situation was always, what is the reality here? What are the facts?

Everyone is in the business of problem solving and decision-making throughout their entire lives. In fact, life is a continual succession of problems, large and small. Your success is largely determined by your effectiveness in solving problems and making good decisions, and your success in these areas is largely determined by the accuracy of the information you have to work with. The more information you have from more sources, the more likely you are to have sufficient facts and details to make decisions that will bring about the desired result.

As a management consultant to many companies over the years, my primary contribution to strategic planning sessions and groups of senior executives has been to help them to ask and answer the hard questions that determine the future of their businesses: Who is your customer? What does your customer consider to be a value? What benefits does your customer pay for when he or she buys your product or service? What is your unique selling proposition? What about your product or service makes it superior to any other product or service in the current marketplace? What is your competitive advantage today? What will it be tomorrow? What should it be? What could it be? What will your customer consider to be of value tomorrow? What steps can you take today to ensure that your products or services are superior to those of your competitors in the markets of tomorrow, next year, and beyond?

These questions force key decision-makers to think through exactly what they offer in the marketplace and what they will have to be offering tomorrow in order to survive and thrive in a greatly changed economic environment. Fully 80 percent of the products and services that people are using today did not exist five years ago. Fully 80 percent of the products and services that people will be using in five years are still being developed as we speak. If you have young children, when they grow up ten or fifteen years from now, they'll be working for companies that do not today exist. They'll be producing and marketing products and services that do not today exist. They'll be using skills, abilities, and knowledge that do not today exist. They'll be doing jobs that don't yet exist and selling to customers and markets that don't yet exist. If your career is going to stretch over the next ten or fifteen years or more, this will be your situation as well. The best way to predict the future is to create it. Your ability to acquire accurate intelligence and information today so that you can make better decisions for tomorrow is as important to your success as any other activity you undertake.

The good news is that your mind is like a muscle. The more you use it, the stronger it becomes. The more you feed your mind with new information and ideas, the better and more capable it becomes at taking in and retaining even more information.

There's a lot of talk today about the fact that incomes have leveled off and sometimes declined for a great number of people. This is true, but only for those who have stopped learning. Almost everything you know about your work will be obsolete within a few years. If you work in the stock market, where information is changing minute by minute, virtually everything you know will be obsolete within a few weeks. You must be continually upgrading your knowledge and intelligence.

I spoke to a woman recently who had taken two years off from her work to travel and upgrade her education. She told me that when she came back, her entire industry had changed so dramatically that she was forced to start over again at the beginning. Nothing that she knew about her industry, the products and services being sold, or the people in it was true after two years; it was almost as if all her previous experience had been for nothing.

The people who continue to get additional information and to upgrade their intelligence and their ability, their knowledge, and their know-how are the most fortunate people in our society. They are seeing their incomes increase anywhere from 8 to 25 percent per year. The men and women whose unique combination of intelligence, ideas, intuition, and abilities enable them to control large corporations and make decisions that affect millions of dollars and thousands of people are some of the highest paid, most respected, and most valued people in the world today.

In America and throughout most of the industrialized world, we live in a meritocracy. This means that you are largely paid on the basis of your merit, your ability to make a valuable contribution to the world around you. In short, you are paid for results. Everything you do that increases your ability to get more and better results that people will pay for increases your value and the amount you receive.

The highest-paid people in America today work an average of fifty-nine hours per week. They read an average of two to three hours per day. They belong to industry, associations, and organizations that continually feed them with current information and ideas on their fields. They attend annual conventions, and they go to every session available that has new insights that can help them to be more effective in getting the results for which they are responsible and for which they're paid.

The Dollar Value of Education

The statistics on the value of higher education over time are remarkable. According to one recent source, a two-year associate's degree typically confers a 25 percent boost and a bachelor's degree a 75 percent boost in lifetime earnings over a high-school diploma. A bachelor's degree holder earns, at the median, $2.8 million over a lifetime, translating into average annual earnings of about $70,000. Master's degree holders earn a median of $3.2 million over their lifetimes, while doctoral degree holders earn $4 million and professional degree holders earn $4.7 million.

Moreover, continual learning is the minimum requirement for success in your field. Since information knowledge in every field is doubling every two to three years, your knowledge has to double every two to three years as well just for you to stay even.

> **Three Types of Learning**
> 1. Maintenance learning
> 2. Growth learning
> 3. Shock learning

Three Types of Learning

There are three different kinds of education that you can acquire, either deliberately or in a random, haphazard fashion: *maintenance learning*, *growth learning*, and *shock learning*.

Maintenance learning refers to keeping current with your field, but this merely keeps you even or stops you from falling behind at a more rapid rate. Many people think that reading an occasional book and keeping current with the magazines and newsletters in their field adds to their education, but this is not entirely the case. It is the same as checking the stock market reports each day to find out the sales prices of various stocks and securities. This information does not add to your knowledge of the companies, the market, or the investment potential of a particular stock. It merely keeps you up to date.

Nevertheless, maintenance learning is essential. It's very similar to light physical exercise. It keeps you at a particular level of fitness but does not increase your level of fitness or improve your conditioning beyond what it already is.

The second type of learning is *growth learning*, which adds knowledge and skills to your repertoire that you did not have before. For example, if you decide to learn to speak Spanish so that you can expand your business opportunities into the Hispanic market, every word, phrase, and sentence that you learn is a form of growth learning. You are acquiring information that enables you to do things that you could not do before. Some of the best thinkers in the world today are producing some of the best material that you can use to improve your life and business. You can acquire this information just by reaching out your hand and picking it up in the form of books, articles, courses, and websites.

The third type of learning is called *shock learning*. This is where something happens that contradicts or reverses a piece of knowledge or understanding that you already have. Shock learning could be extremely valuable if you act upon it. In his book *Innovation and Entrepreneurship*, Peter Drucker says that the primary sources of innovation and breakthroughs in a company are the unexpected success or the unexpected failure: something happens that is completely inconsistent with the expectation, with what should have happened. This shock can give insights that can enable you either to take advantage of a major change in the marketplace or guard against a serious reversal.

Unfortunately, most people are creatures of habit. When something unexpected happens, they choose to ignore it in favor of the old information, with which they are more comfortable. This is why most major breakthroughs in business and industry come from outside that particular industry. The Rand Corporation invented the computer, but IBM took the concept and turned it into the most successful commercial enterprise in computers in the world. The Xerox research laboratories invented the personal computer, but they concluded that it had no place in the marketplace of photocopiers that Xerox dominated. Companies like Apple, IBM, and

Dell took the personal computer and made it a multibillion-dollar worldwide industry. There's a phenomenon in business and industry called *NIH* or "not invented here."

Many companies, organizations, and individuals are completely closed to any idea that they did not think of personally. If it was not invented by them, they conclude that it can be of no value to them. The head of a major British business industrial group was once quoted as saying that only British ideas about business are of any value to British companies; nothing coming from America or any other land has any application to the British situation. This attitude can be fatal to a business.

Americans, on the other end, have a wonderful quality that has made this the most dynamic nation in the world. Americans are extremely pragmatic. Americans do not care where the idea comes from. Their only concern is, does it work? Take a new medicine that will cure an illness for which there was previously no cure. Americans do not care who invented the medicine; they only want to know whether or not it works. If it works, they will take it and use it faster than virtually any other national culture or group.

American entrepreneurs and businesses have another quality that has given the United States leadership in technology: they are willing to take a new idea and run with it immediately, fixing it up and improving it as they move along. Major industrial competitors in Japan and Germany are so concerned about making a mistake that they will spend years perfecting a new piece of technology before they bring it to the marketplace. In some cases, this works in their favor and they develop a tremendous reputation for quality, but in the world of high tech, it is hurting them tremendously: by the time they've perfected a technological innovation or breakthrough, the Americans have already brought it to the market and seized the high ground in the minds of the customers.

In his book *Real Time,* aerospace leader Norman Augustine talks about the importance of speed in an era of rapid change. He points out that the key to business success today is contained in the term *time to market.* You could have the best idea in the world, but if somebody else beats you to the marketplace with it, that company takes the high ground.

In their work on positioning, Al Ries and Jack Trout show that the company that gets into the market first with a new product innovation or idea usually becomes permanently associated with that new product or service. Competitors that come into the market afterwards run the risk of being perceived as imitator or copycats.

Knowledge is the primary source of value in our world today, and your ability to acquire the critical knowledge you need and apply it rapidly to get better and faster results for which people will pay you is the key to breaking through any success barriers that may be in front of you.

Many companies are now taking stock of their intellectual capital. They are appointing knowledge executives or knowledge experts to locate and identify the different forms of knowledge that exist within an organization. Today the primary assets of any organization walk out the door at five o'clock. In fact, your company could burn to the ground tomorrow, but as long as your staff with their brain power survived, you could walk across the street and start over again the next day. Everything is brainpower, and your ability to acquire more and more useful brainpower is virtually unlimited.

> **Three Forms of Business Knowledge**
> 1. Specific skills and abilities
> 2. Knowledge of products and processes
> 3. Knowledge of customers, markets, suppliers, and the way the industry works

Three Forms of Knowledge

Three forms of knowledge give value to individuals and organizations. The first form is contained in specific skills and abilities, the core competencies that enable you to get the results you are paid for. Your most valuable asset is your earning ability: your ability to apply your intelligence and energy to your world to produce goods and services that people want, need, and are willing to pay for. Everything you do throughout your life is aimed at increasing and enhancing your earning ability.

People who make large salaries are not necessarily smarter than many people who make smaller salaries, but they have strategically developed their earning abilities to a very high level, and they have learned how to sell those abilities at a high price in a competitive marketplace.

You must resolve to be among the top 10 percent in your field in terms of the specific skills and abilities that you need to do your job. If you're in sales, your goal must be to excel at the critical success factors of selling, such as prospecting, establishing rapport, identifying problems and needs, presenting your product or service as the best solution to them, answering objections, closing the sale, and getting referrals and resales.

If you are a company owner or manager, you must excel at assembling the necessary resources to bring competitive products to your market in a timely fashion and at a price that people are willing to pay. You must excel at picking the right people to work for you, delegating to them, supervising them properly, and getting maximum results from your team.

Whatever you do, there are a series of critical skills whose sum total adds up to the amount that you can charge for your services in a competitive marketplace. Sometimes one additional skill can greatly increase your value.

The second type of knowledge that is a major source of value for individuals and corporations is the knowledge of the company's products and processes. Remember, the primary asset of any company resides between the ears of the key people in that organization. Many people carry "key man insurance," which covers them for millions of dollars should a key person pass away suddenly. These companies recognize that the loss of a key person can be very harmful to an organization. The more you know about your company's products and processes, what goes into them and how the company operates internally, the more valuable you are.

The key to success in every field of intelligence and knowledge is to overlearn. Never assume that you already know all that you need to know. Always assume that there is an enormous amount still to be learned.

The third type of knowledge that represents extraordinary value for a company is the knowledge of customers, markets, suppliers, and the way the industry works. This type of knowledge can be worth a fortune to an organization. This is why companies will often pay enormous salaries to hire away highly competent people from competitors. They are buying the brainpower and experience of those individuals rather than taking the months and years to develop that brainpower and experience in someone else.

Here is a little-known rule that is important for you to be aware of: good people are free. Good people don't cost anything. Good people actually contribute far more in net profitability than they take out in salary. A company can hire all the good people it wants all day long, and it can pay them anything that it takes to get them to come over, because in the final analysis, they don't cost the company anything at all. They contribute net bottom line dollars to the organization. This is why the best companies have the best people. The second-best companies have the second-best people, and the third-best companies are on their way out of business, because they simply cannot compete with the first- and second-best companies.

Continual training and development is so important for every individual and every organization because it is the only way that you can upgrade your human skills aside from buying the skills in the open market. The most profitable companies spend the most on training. The second most profitable companies spend the second greatest amount on training, and the companies that are on their way out of business are always talking about training but never do it. The intellectual capital you carry around between your ears makes you an extremely valuable resource. At the same time, your earning ability is becoming obsolete at an increasingly faster rate because of the explosion of information and technology.

You owe it to yourself, your family, your company, and your future to be a learning machine: you must be continually gobbling up new ideas and information from all sources so that you can get into the top 10 percent and stay there.

One good idea is all you need to start a fortune, but you can only be assured of getting that one good idea by continually bombarding your mind with ideas of all kinds, from all sources. Every change or improvement in your life will come about as a result of your mind colliding with a new idea of some kind. This new idea will give you a different perspective and cause you to see things in a different way. As a result, you'll take different actions and get different results.

The law of probability applies to ideas and information: the more ideas and information you surround yourself with, the more likely you will be to have the right idea at the right time in the right situation to make the right decision.

Integrative Intelligence

I've already discussed the principle of integrative intelligence. The people who rise to the top of every organization are the ones who have the greatest accumulation of ideas and knowledge available with which to make better decisions with more positive potential consequences. You must become an idea sponge. You should organize your life so that ideas are continually coming at you from all directions.

You begin with very clear goals and objectives for yourself and for every part of your life. One goal must be to earn an excellent living, to be paid at the top of the income scale that is possible in your industry, if not higher. Another goal should be to double your income within the next two or three years and then double it again and again. Countless thousands of people who are less talented than you are doing this on a regular basis, so you can as well. You then determine what kind of results you will have to get and what kind of contribution you will have to make in order to be worth the kind of money that you aspire to earn.

Look around you. Who else is making the kind of money that you want to make? What are they doing differently from you? If you're not sure, go and ask them. They will always tell you. I have found that successful people are always willing to help other people to be successful. If you call them, write to them, or take them out to lunch or coffee and ask them, they will tell you what to do more of and what to do less of. They will tell you the key turning points in their own lives. They will tell you the books they read, the audios they listened to, and the insights that they have gained from experience. Whatever your goals, realize that you will have to learn and develop expertise in a new subject area for you to achieve a goal that you have never achieved before.

Whenever you set a new goal, you ask yourself, what will I have to learn to achieve this goal? Dedicate yourself to lifelong learning. The future belongs to the competent, not to the well-meaning. The future belongs to people who are exceptionally good at what they do. Many people think that as soon as they get the job they want, they will work hard and become extremely good at that job. But excellent performance is the key to advancement and promotion: only when you become really good at your current level will you be promoted upward to a higher level. Until you get good, get better, and become the best at your current job, you don't move. The people who are working away on themselves will pass you by on either side.

Here are the rules for continual learning and personal development. They require willpower, self-discipline, and self-control until you have developed the habit of continual learning. Once you've developed the habit, the rewards and benefits you'll enjoy will far outweigh the efforts and the energy that you invest.

First, remember that reading is to the mind as exercise is to the body. Read for at least one hour every day in your chosen field.

Read the best books being written by the best people. Ask for recommendations from other successful people, get those books, and read them. When you read, take careful notes, underline with a red pen, and make all kinds of stars and exclamation points in the margins so that you can find key points when you reread the material. After you've read a good book, sit down with a spiral notebook and write out the most important things that you have learned. You'll be amazed at how many of these ideas are then transferred into your long-term memory and become available for you when you need them later.

Subscribe to and read all the magazines in your field. Keep current with what is going on. Read the newsletters and the parts of the newspapers that apply to your area of activity. After all, one key piece of information at a critical time can make all the difference to you. Take all the training you can get, attend every course that comes along that can give you additional knowledge and skills that you need to lead your field.

All education is free, in the sense that if it's helpful to your life and to your career, your return on investment will be ten, twenty, even thirty times your investment in the learning experience. Listen to audio programs in your car. A six-hour audio program usually contains the best ideas of thirty to fifty books on a variety of subjects. By listening to audio programs, you turn driving time into learning time; you turn your car into a university on wheels.

Above all, remember that continual learning saves time, energy, and life. It enables you to achieve far more in a shorter period of time than any other way. Continual learning puts you in complete control of your life and your future. It expands your freedom of choice and increases your opportunities in all directions. It increases your income and improves your lifestyle. It builds self-reliance, self-confidence, and self-esteem. An ongoing commitment to gathering the central intelligence of your life and your work will make you a master of change rather than a victim. Continual learning will give you the ammunition you need to blast through any success barriers that may be standing in your way.

Key Points

- Your ability to upgrade your knowledge and skills is critical to your success.
- The I3 model of power: information, intelligence, and action.
- +Refuse to settle for apparent or assumed facts.
- Everyone is in the business of problem solving and decision-making.
- Your mind is like a muscle. The more you use it, the stronger it becomes.
- You are largely paid on the basis of your ability to make a valuable contribution.
- Continual learning is the minimum requirement for success.
- Three types of learning: maintenance learning, growth learning, and shock learning.
- Knowledge is the primary source of value today.
- Good people don't cost anything. They contribute far more in net profitability than they take out in salary.
- Organize your life so that ideas are continually coming at you from all directions.
- The future belongs to people who are exceptionally good at what they do.
- Reading is to the mind as exercise is to the body.

* * *

Life's a battle, we constantly hear. As we've seen from the lessons above, you can win this battle by applying these simple but powerful strategies that have brought victory to great military leaders such as Alexander the Great, Erwin Rommel, and General Norman Schwarzkopf. Using the ideas outlined here, you can defeat your worst enemies—fear and doubt—and attain everything you've ever dreamed of, and more.

www.ingramcontent.com/pod-product-compliance
Lightning Source LLC
Chambersburg PA
CBHW072212070526
44585CB00015B/1298